Enough Is Enough!

Exposing the Education System After Their Failed Attempt to Label and Drug My Son

by Barbie Rivera

For more information, visit
https://BarbieRivera.com

Brilliance Learning Press

Book cover and layout by Brilliance Learning Press

First edition 2024

Print: ISBN: 978-1-957128-06-1

eBook: ISBN: 978-1-957128-07-8

Reviews

The book, *Enough is Enough!* by Barbie Rivera, should be required reading in every college and university that has an education program.
M.H. Parent with a Master's Degree in Education

A truly revelatory book for anyone who cares about this country's future. This chilling story of how America's literacy rate has been deliberately and methodically destroyed over time will leave you speechless. Whether you have children or not, this is a must-read.
N.G. 20-year High School English & Math Teacher

Barbie Rivera exposes the education system in an enlightening and inspiring way. She makes this difficult subject easily understandable and she does it effectively. What I appreciate the most is that she speaks only from her personal experiences and she's not trying to be someone she's not. I was never once bored with this book and couldn't put it down.
C.G. High School 9th Grader

For any parent who has been bewildered, affronted and horrified with attempts to label and degrade their child by so-called experts, read *Enough is Enough!* NOW. Become aware of what you are facing and learn how to say NO to drugging and YES to education.
F.D.S. Jr. NAACP California-Hawaii State Conference Children's Task Force Committee

This book exposes the truth and how our public education system is deteriorating and how our country's future is at risk. This book is a must read if you want to know about the current public education system and what to look out for.
I.Q. 11th Grade High School Student

This book resonated with me in a direct and personal way. This book tells the glaring truth of the aggression used by "experts" who think they know more than parents, students, or teachers. This book must be heard.

P.P. Certified Teacher with Two Master's Degrees

Enough is Enough! shows precisely what is wrong with the over-professionalized approach to the care and education of young people and how this works against a human, common sense approach. The fact that Barbie is a mother without a degree or formal teacher training is powerfully significant and will inspire readers/parents/teachers to think independently with confidence.

D.H. Children's Health Defense Ireland

This book tells a remarkable story of dedication, perseverance, research, and great outcomes. Thank goodness I was able to teach before Common Core methodology was introduced in schools. Who in the world would teach this way?

R.K. Twice Voted Teacher of the Year Atlanta, Georgia, Inducted into the Kermit Blosser Baseball Hall of Fame in 2020 and the Georgia Dugout Club Hall of Fame

I can relate to the author and her son as something similar happened to me with my oldest child. Great book. 100% recommend reading it.

A.Q. Father & Business Owner

Dedication

This book is dedicated to my children Damon, Morgan, Adam, Michael and Thor. And to my private school staff who have become my second family.

I love you all.

Table of Contents

Note to Reader

In 1991, a teacher told me that my six-year-old son was "mentally handicapped" and would need medication to learn.

I disagreed.

My son hit all the previous toddler milestones such as first words, first steps and potty training. He was bright, funny, honest, exceptionally well-behaved, respectful, spoke two languages and could draw quite well. He was a good big brother to his three siblings, helped with chores, built tents out of blankets, climbed trees, ran in the rain, and did all the things little boys do.

I thought he'd ace school.

He didn't.

Just two weeks into first grade, it was determined that my beautiful boy was "mentally disabled" and his only hope of learning was psychotropic medications that he would most likely need for the rest of his life.

This is my story of saving my son.

Every word of what I have written is true. The documents cited have actually passed through my hands. The questionable curriculum or questionable school assignments mentioned were all viewed directly by me (not from an internet search).

Any children I write about are those who I have actually worked with (names have been changed for privacy purposes). The parents I speak of are people I have actually communicated with (again, names have been changed). Some stories have happy endings and some don't.

Some of my viewpoints may be frowned upon by modern experts, who spent years in universities, hold multiple certificates and have sadly become the "authorities" on education who are determining that a large population of children are unable to learn. I am not speaking to these or any "experts."

I am certain that my grammar will not pass the scrutiny of an English professor. I am telling a story, not trying to earn a Ph.D.

Finally, I don't use big words because I don't know any.

I am sharing my story.

This is about saving my child from being labeled and drugged.

Part One

Chapter 1

Introduction

Before I launch into the topic of this book of why I chose to home-school, I feel it is necessary (or at least polite) to familiarize the reader with who I am and what the circumstances were that led me to homeschooling and ultimately opening my own private school.

I have divided this book into sections: 1) an introduction to myself and my son, 2) a hard look at the current education system, and finally, 3) what I did to ensure my son was educated (not medicated or indoctrinated).

Mayflower Descendant

My family tree goes back to the Mayflower in 1620. John Howland was a young, 20-something servant, working in exchange for passage to the New World. During a storm, a rogue wave hit the Mayflower, throwing John overboard into the freezing Atlantic. Most people would have frozen to death or drowned.

Not John.

He managed to grab onto a rope and though getting battered by freezing waves and pelted with rain, he held on long enough to be pulled aboard to safety. He overcame impossible odds and survived.

I am a direct descendant of John Howland from my mother's side of the family. I like to think that some of his determination was passed down to me.

John Howland was an original signer of the Mayflower Compact. He married Elizabeth Tilley and had ten children, all of whom survived to adulthood. Today there are said to be over two million direct descendants of John Howland.

My grandmother had 13 children (the first two passed away in childhood). My mother was number 11. My mother and her siblings produced 45 grandchildren. The number of great-grandchildren more than doubled this figure and the great-great-great grandchildren added even more.

My grandmother remained alert and sassy right to the end of her 97 years. At the time of her passing, our family was five generations strong, with a headcount of 101 total grandchildren.

Western-Southern's Insurance Women's Baseball Team and How My Parents Met

My mother Marian and her older sister Betty worked at Western-Southern Insurance in Cincinnati, Ohio. They were both key members of the company's women's baseball team. The coach took his job very seriously and was all business, giving his team the reputation of being one of the strongest in the league, winning one (if not more) championships.

However, in order for my mother and Betty to play baseball, my grandfather insisted that his daughters be fully chaperoned for each practice and every game. Enter my mother's three older brothers, Herb, Frank and Robert. (Robert was nicknamed "Speed" as an inside joke.

My mother's brothers: Herb, Charlie, Robert and Frank

Apparently, he was really slow. Joke or not, I actually grew up thinking it was his real name.) My mother's brothers took turns accompanying their sisters to games, taking pride in their sisters' skills on the field.

I do not know the order of how the team fell apart, or who did what first, but I do know that my uncles were completely responsible for the dismantling of the women's baseball team which became a full feature in the local newspaper.

The problem with women's baseball and employment in the late 1940s was that once a woman got married she was fired from her job and let go from the team. Women were supposed to focus on their family. This was how things were done in the late 1940s.

One by one my mother's brothers (the chaperones) began to marry members of the women's baseball team. One by one the increasingly frustrated coach ended up losing seasoned players to the Hamlin family.

The coach did not know there was another Hamlin boy. When Charlie, the youngest, showed up to watch a game the coach factually ordered him off the grounds, banning him from coming anywhere near his team or attending any future games. The story of the coach's frustration of losing his team to the Hamlin boys ran in the local paper.

But the disruption to the team did not stop there.

My Uncle Frank invited his

Pictured are Betty (left), standing with her sister (my mother), and Marian (right); Alma (rear)and Clara (front) both married into the family, along with Laura (not pictured).

- 17 -

Navy buddy, Jerry, to a game. Jerry took a liking to Marian. They got married, and there went another member of the team. And that is the story of how my parents met.

Fun fact: My Aunt Betty, the final Hamlin female on the team, was offered a position on the national women's team featured in the movie *A League of Their Own*. One of my cousins has the recruitment letter signed by Jimmy Dugan (played by Tom Hanks). My grandfather did not allow Betty to join the team as having a young woman travel unescorted from city to city to play baseball would have been scandalous. My uncles were all starting families of their own so were unable to chaperone.

Cincinnati

I was born and raised in Cincinnati, Ohio. I am number four of five children. Within a minute of my birth, doctors informed my mother that I had a heart murmur and would most likely need open-heart surgery before my tenth birthday.

Unfortunately, my mother was drugged during my birth (as was the custom in 1964) so had no recall of hearing about any heart condition. When I got a checkup as a toddler, the doctor told my mother heart surgery could not wait and needed to be scheduled immediately. My mother thought he was joking. According to her, I was very active and showed no signs of having anything wrong.

A follow-up exam confirmed that without immediate action, I did not have long to live.

I cannot imagine the stress my parents were thrown into. Besides the fact that I (a toddler) needed life-saving surgery, both of my parents had to work to make ends meet, and they had four other children, including my brother just shy of his first birthday, to look after. And it was just before Christmas.

Though small, I have memories from this time period. I remember my Aunt Betty coming by almost every night after work. (She was going to babysit and help manage the house while I was hospitalized.) The neighbor, Jackie, took care of my baby brother during the day and ensured everyone got off to school. There was lots of planning. Lots of movement. Lots of random people doing various things.

My older brothers, who usually enjoyed teasing me, were told firmly by my father to leave me alone. It was the first time I heard my father speak in this tone, and it was my first hint that there was something amiss.

My parents did their best to prepare me for surgery. The night before going to the hospital, they sat me on the dining room table to talk. Sitting on the table. No one ever sat on the dining room table in my house, yet here were my mother and father, both seated in chairs looking at me, fully aware I was sitting on the table and neither seemed angry. I was little, but I knew something serious was going on.

They told me that my heart was not beating properly and needed to be fixed. I was shown photos of a heart from a large Human Anatomy book. They ran a finger around my rib cage to show where my scar would be. They told me I'd be in a hospital for weeks but should be home in time for Santa. They showed me new pajamas, a new toothbrush, a new stuffed animal. My mother showed me a dress she made with a giraffe on the front.

I liked the dress, pajamas and toy, but my three-year-old self was not having any of the rest of it. I felt my chest and my heart seemed to be beating just fine.

A night before I was hospitalized, my parents decided to use my love of the Monkees to get me to understand the surgery. I was told that the band lived in my body and that the drummer (Micky Dolenz) continually played

A few weeks before open-heart surgery. Front: Me, Doug, David. Back: Dennis and Vicki.

the wrong beat and needed to get back on track. A doctor needed to open me up, straighten Micky out and all would be good. For some reason, this made sense to me.

The surgical team actually had me point out Micky Dolenz from a Monkees magazine. They wanted to make sure they did not "spank" the wrong band member. I was taken to surgery with a Tiger Beat magazine in my bed.

Surgery took 13 hours but was a success; recovery a nightmare (probably worse for my parents), but true to my father's word, after a three-week hospital stay, I arrived home just in time for Christmas. I was taped from my hips to my armpits. I had 158 stitches, kidney stones, was unable to take deep breaths, cough, laugh or move, but I was home in time for Santa.

It took months to fully recover. By summer I was back to being an active child, running around shirtless in backyard sprinklers, showing off a rather impressive scar.

I do not plan to do a deep dive into my childhood, but there are a few incidents I'd like to relay, even if only for the humor.

Meeting My Parent's Idol: Pete Rose

Seeing how baseball is what brought my parents together, I will share the true story of how Pete Rose ruined my life. I will start by saying Pete Rose actually did nothing wrong. He was nothing but gracious and nice to me when we met. However, due to my surgery, I was an automatic member of a "Cincinnati heart club." I do not remember its official name, but it was a Cincinnati thing or a Children's Hospital thing. Children with various heart conditions were automatically part of a "club." We'd get invited to movie outings with family (where popcorn and drinks were free) and we could attend other events throughout the year. Sometimes these events were in a group, and sometimes events involved only one child.

For my fourth birthday, I was invited to go to a Cincinnati Reds game as Pete Rose's personal guest. I met Pete outside of his locker room where he autographed a poster, a bat, a baseball card and wrote Happy Birthday Barbara on a baseball.

Outside his locker room there was a large bowl of Bazooka gum. I asked for one; he dumped the bowl into a bag and gave it all to me. For our photo, he was careful, picking me up awkwardly from under my arms. We took a picture, I got a kiss on the cheek and he promised to hit me a home run. Very nice man. (And he did hit that promised home run!)

My father hung the autographed poster and baseball card in my toy nook, a would-be butler's pantry connecting the kitchen to the dining room. This way, guests could easily view it when stopping by. And for days I was asked to tell the story of our meeting over and over, which made me feel good.

A week went by and the photo of Pete Rose and me arrived. Everyone was thrilled to see me being held by this local celebrity. My parents' favorite REDs player. Barbara and Pete Rose. Pete Rose and Barbara. It was a big, big deal.

I, on the other hand, was absolutely mortified. The way Pete Rose was holding me caused my dress to go up, putting my underwear on full display. Cropping photos wasn't a thing at the time so I just had to live with it.

While the adults were oohing and aahing over the photo, I decided to get even with Pete Rose. I grabbed my least favorite crayon (orange), went to my toy nook and began defacing my autographed Pete Rose poster by drawing horns on his head and coloring in his teeth. I ripped the baseball card into pieces. I turned my attention to the base-ball, but my father grabbed it first. He tried to soothe me, saying my underwear looked like bloomers that matched the dress. His words did not help. I was upset and determined to stay that way.

Later, when my parents would watch the Reds on TV, they'd all chant,

"*Get a hit, Pete!*" when he'd come up to bat. If one listened closely, they'd have heard me say under my breath: "*Don't get a hit, underwear man!*"

Artistic Support and Good Advice

In the fall of this same year, my brothers and sister went back to school. At age four, I was too young to start kindergarten, leaving my mom home with me and my little brother who was almost two. I had four passions: my Barbie dolls, looking at books, the new family puppy, Boots (a beagle mix), and drawing. I loved to draw and would do it for hours.

A family friend and award-winning architect, Gene Hunt, lived a few blocks away. Gene had longish hair, wore Converse and drove a Corvette. His wife dressed like a fashionable hippie, and his home was full of odd sculptures and art. Gene had three teenagers, who were friends with my older siblings.

Gene was very supportive of my art. He said I had a unique style. To support my talent, he would bring me chalk and ask me to draw on the sidewalk. Or he'd buy me crayons and provide scrap paper from his job.

One afternoon he stopped by with a present. He gave me a little desk. The kind that has an attached chair and chalkboard top that opens for storage. The alphabet and numbers 0 to 9 appeared in glossy yellow print across the surface. Each figure had numbered arrows that showed the correct sequence for forming each letter and number.

Gene said that all artists need a space to work from. I now had one.

From this gift came simple advice that instantly improved my ability to draw.

My mother, who had her hands full with my baby brother and wanted to keep me busy, said: "*Barbara, if you learn to write the alphabet and numbers exactly as they look on your desk, you will be able to draw anything. Everything you draw is made of lines. Trees, castles, clouds—they are all formed with lines. Practice writing the lines of letters and numbers and you'll be able to draw anything you want.*"

I sat at my desk for hours writing letters and numbers on the chalk-board desktop. It took me a week or so to master the alphabet and numbers. The number "5" was the trickiest, but with practice I got there.

The ability to correctly form numbers and letters in sequence while focusing on controlling a line had a huge impact on my ability to draw. Huge. Soon I was able to draw things around the house, such as lamps, chairs, pots and pans. My mother would move my desk to a window so I could draw snow or trees. I started drawing people, houses, and my dog.

The encouragement that I got from home regarding my drawings set the stage for me excelling at school. A year later, when I started kinder-garten at McKinley Elementary in Cincinnati's East End, my ability to write and draw impressed my teacher very much. She said that my penmanship was more like a second grader than someone just starting school.

In first grade, my teacher Mrs. Rudd raved about a "pie" I drew to go along with a new vocabulary word. She sent me to show the teacher across the hall who said the pie looked so real she could almost smell it. My mother received a phone call commenting on how good my art was.

This drawing of a pie caused such a positive commotion that I kept it (and still have it to this day). Honestly, it is a very simple drawing. The take-away to this is that a few kind words and a positive phone call home was very encouraging to a first-grade me.

Despite being located in a low-income area, I thought McKinley was a fantastic school. My parents were very happy, too. I loved school. I liked my teachers. And school loved me. This is about as ideal as it gets in terms of a learning environment.

A Reading Assignment That Ended Up Changing Everything in My Adult Life

Fast forward to fourth grade. Mrs. Kennedy was a wonderful teacher. (She looked and acted just like the character Claire Huxtable from *The*

Cosby Show). Her classroom was very large, with big windows where we could see rain, sun and snow. She was organized, knew her subjects well and did not assign homework. She decorated her room for each holiday, giving her class the task of making paper chains or lanterns from colorful paper.

It was very clear that she enjoyed her profession very much. She seemed to have as much fun teaching as we did learning.

It was a cold November day when the principal, Mr. Glenn, (exact image of the old man from the movie *Up*) entered our classroom telling Mrs. Kennedy of a problem he needed solved. I am sure this exchange had been fully rehearsed prior, but here it is:

Mr. Glenn: "*Mrs. Kennedy, the teachers and I think the main hallway to the office is drab and boring. We are all too busy to do anything about it. I do have an idea that I'd like to run by you.*"

Mrs. Kennedy: "*What do you have in mind, Mr. Glenn?*"

Mr. Glenn: "*Do you think Barbara could be put in charge of decorating the bulletin boards for Thanksgiving, then Christmas? I'll supply poster board, construction paper, glue and plenty of markers. Barbara can get help from her playground buddies.*"

Mrs. Kennedy: "*I think this is a wonderful idea.*"

And just like that my friends and I were given an hour at the end of each day to work on making decorations for the main school hallway. We did a feast for Thanksgiving, a large Santa (with a cotton ball beard) for Christmas and so on. We did the Cincinnati skyline and Riverfront Stadium in honor of the Reds when baseball season started.

I remember my mother giving me tissue paper and teaching me how to make paper flowers. We glued said flowers on our "Welcome Spring" poster giving a 3D effect and you'd have thought we just painted the *Mona Lisa* as the principal and teachers all commented how good our art was, using words like "festive" and "welcoming." The principal even called my mother (and my friends' mothers) to say how lucky McKinley was to have such talented artists as students.

The work was never criticized. No one pointed out the mistakes or errors. No one said, "*You went out of line here and here....*" Trust me, the art looked like nine-year-olds did it and was probably a disaster—we never used a ruler when drawing buildings and I remember my Easter Bunny looking more like a rhino than a cute fuzzy rabbit. However, the quality of art was not the point. The point was that a group of fourth graders were engaged on monthly art projects and felt like kings and queens at school. Seriously, even the school janitors would tell us how lovely the halls looked thanks to our artwork.

McKinley Elementary School Cincinnati, Ohio

It was during fourth grade reading class that I encountered a story that literally haunted me. One, I found the story unbelievable, and two, it was absolutely true.

Our reading books contained a collection of stories that were broken down into daily assignments with a question-and-answer quiz occurring each Friday. A typical class involved Mrs. Kennedy calling on students to read parts of our textbook out loud. Mrs. Kennedy would explain words or stop to discuss various characters and events.

The title of the story for that week was "Set Me Free" and it had an illustration of a little girl giving an emotional hug to a woman. Both were dressed in old-fashioned clothing.

The first paragraph went something like: Imagine you are cold but do not have a word to express this. Imagine you are hungry, but you are unable to tell someone you need food. Imagine the sky is three different colors, but you only see black....

The story was about Helen Keller and how an illness left her totally blind and deaf when she was just a baby, resulting in her being unable to see, hear and speak. As a person who overcame a serious health condition, I could relate to some degree. The key though: I overcame my condition.

Helen did not.

Every word of every paragraph that was read seemed to reach out of the book and slap me in the face. What would I do if I were unable to hear music? (At the time, my brother was really into Jimi Hendrix and would show me various chords on the guitar.) Living in silence without Elton John, Jimi Hendrix or any number of artists my brother listened to was unthinkable.

What if I would never hear my father's or mother's voice again?

What would I do if I could not see? I had a collection of 11 stuffed animals on my bed and I loved each and every one of them: their eyes, their colors, some dressed in clothes. I lay in bed at night with my eyes closed, feeling the stuffed animals (as if I were blind) and the experience was not the same. I needed my eyes.

What would I do if I did not have a language? If I did not have words? What if I could not talk to my dog or tell my little brother a joke? I needed my voice.

The reading book went on to say that at age six, completely cut off from the world, Helen had the mannerisms of an animal. She was out of control, wild, dirty, and unmanageable.

Her parents considered putting her in an asylum as she was a danger to herself and others. Asylums were the professional standard of treatment of this time period. Thankfully, the parents chose to hire a tutor, Anne Sullivan, to work with Helen at home. Anne herself was barely 20.

Helen hated her teacher from the start; however, Anne persisted, teaching Helen how to use a fork and spoon and fold a napkin. The teacher had Helen feel the sign language alphabet with her hands. Helen resisted, punched, kicked, but her teacher persisted.

One day (only a month after the teacher first arrived) Helen made the connection. The miracle happened at a water pump where Helen recalled the word "wa-wa." (Her pre-illness word for "water.") She actually spoke.

Helen discovered that the objects and people that she could not see and could not hear were represented by words. These words were contained in the sign language Anne was teaching. For the first time in her life, Helen could effectively communicate. I cried in class reading about this.

The story ended on that miracle, but Mrs. Kennedy explained that Helen went on to be the first blind and deaf person to earn a college degree with honors. She won an Academy Award for a documentary about her life. And a few years before she died, she was awarded the Presidential Medal of Freedom, which is our nation's highest civilian honor.

My teacher explained that Helen changed the world for a community of deaf and blind people. She and her tutor Anne were an inspiration to both the disabled and non-disabled.

I believe this was the only time our class applauded a story.

During the discussion time, a boy asked Mrs. Kennedy, *"How did Anne know Helen would learn?"*

Mrs. Kennedy answered, *"She loved her enough to teach her. The same way I love you."*

Powerful.

Little did I know then, but Mrs. Kennedy, Mr. Glenn, Helen Keller and Anne Sullivan would all end up giving me the courage to take my life in a completely unexpected direction.

Chapter 2

Damon

I had just turned 20 years old when Damon was born. I get it. I was young, maybe too young, but my age (or lack of age) had no bearing on the intensity of meeting my first baby. His eyes. His mouth. His toes. His fingers. His newborn smell. The way he stretched. The noises he made. How he enjoyed being swaddled after a warm bath. His smile.

The fact that this beautiful baby was mine seemed unreal. Meeting him after months of carrying him was unreal. Being a mother was unreal. This little boy completely had my heart. A true example of "love at first sight."

Damon was the first grandchild for my then husband's side of the family. Damon adored his Cuban grandparents, Pipo and Mima (pronounced Pee-po and Mee-ma) and his aunt and uncles. They sang him Spanish lullabies, fed him rice and beans and laughed at all of his antics.

My parents, though 1,000 miles away, adored Damon as well. My mother sent him homemade clothes, toys and blankets. When my parents first met Damon, he was five months old. I don't think my mother let go of him. As was tradition, my father, with his deep voice, took his grandson around the house, showing him how light switches worked or where the kitchen towels were kept.

Damon grew up surrounded by people who loved him, giving him the care and attention all children rightfully deserve.

By the time Damon was six, he had a sister, a brother from my second marriage (don't judge) and was about to become an older brother again, as I was pregnant.

Damon was bright, not just smart, but bright. He'd ask questions, hold conversations, he showed interest in animals and nature. He was funny, creative, fluent in English and Spanish and was exceptionally well-behaved.

He wanted to grow up to be a policeman and be a starter in the NBA, which were fine career choices, supported by all who knew him.

At home, Damon would sit next to the baby carrier, telling his baby brother stories or knock-knock jokes. He would pat my belly and give a nice hello to his other brother, Michael, who was not yet born. Damon went on sleepovers, played Batman, went fishing, helped set the table. He liked LEGO® bricks, puzzles, board games and drawing superheroes. Damon did all the normal things boys do and he got along nicely with most everyone.

He never had a temper tantrum or threw a fit. I don't recall ever raising my voice at him. Damon was easy.

He was nervous about starting school, but excited. He had new clothes, light-up sneakers, a cool lunchbox, backpack and slick haircut. He had an abundance of school supplies, with Ninja Turtle erasers he could share. He was ready.

I imagined his teacher calling to tell me how well-mannered he was and what a good example he set. Saying she'd take a classroom full of students like him. In turn, I could picture Damon wanting to give his teacher a special coffee mug or some chocolates he saw at the grocery store.

I looked forward to getting a phone call telling me a "pie" he drew in spelling looked good enough to eat or that he was asked to decorate a bulletin board.

I expected Damon to have the same experience I did. Thinking that Damon would excel. Be admired. Make friends. Have fun.

I expected him to love school.

Unfortunately, that is not what happened.

Not even close.

On the first day of school, Damon came home with homework he could not do. He had to read a short story and answer questions. The story opened with: "The curious raccoon scampered up the tree...."

I do not think I am one of those parents that "over-coddles" their child, but how could my son be expected to "read and answer questions" when he did not actually know how to read? What happened to recognizing letters and knowing their sounds as the first step in learning to read? Where were the workbooks with pages and pages showing a picture of a dog, dish or daisy with a space for the student to trace the letter *d* next to the images that start with the *d* sound?

What happened to learning three-letter words such as sun, pig, mop, ten, before we get to "curious raccoons" which are words belonging in the second, if not third grade?

How could my son be expected to "write complete sentences" when he did not know what a "sentence" was—not because he was dumb— he just did not know.

And finally, who assigns first graders homework?

Like a "good mom," I sat with my son and helped him for over an hour to get his work done. He was frustrated but we got it done. I was frustrated, but we got it done. My other three children, all under the age of four were frustrated, too. They needed me, but I was rooted to the dining room table "helping" Damon with homework.

On day three, Damon came home in tears. He had a paper with a red **F** written on it. The **F** was about the size of my hand. He was embarrassed to show me, but I had to sign the paper and return it to school.

The directions on the paper asked the student to draw a circle around words that started with *sn* sound. As there was a drawing of a pre-circled snowman, my son (who could not read the directions) thought he was supposed to circle everything that was cold. Damon had no idea why he got an **F** and was devastated.

I disagreed with the assignment as it covered letter combinations before he knew the individual sounds of letters. I was no teacher, but logic tells me that one must walk before one skateboards. In this case, one would have to know individual letter sounds of *s* and *n* before being able to grasp combination *sn*.

My son was not questioned about his work or given a chance to re-do it once he knew what to do.

I disagreed with the size of the **F** given to him. The teacher had to see he was in tears over the grade. She had to at least know he may not be happy with getting an **F** in the first week of school. She had to know that giving him a packet of work and expecting him to follow written directions when he could not read was completely unrealistic and, dare I say, irresponsible on her part.

The homework load increased as did the grade level required to do the work. Everything was accelerated. Damon was expected to identify nouns and verbs in sentences. He had to show the correct use of a semi-colon (something most adults cannot do).

There was no logical progression of arithmetic, just a jumble of random skills, poorly explained, thrown at him. He would have addition on Monday, fractions on Tuesday, multiplication, counting coins and telling time on Wednesday, and so on. Nothing was presented in a step-by-step progression. Nothing was repeated so that the skill could actually be mastered. Games were not offered as a fun way to reinforce ideas.

When I was growing up, we did not start learning grammar until fourth or fifth grade. We were permitted to become fully familiar with English before tackling the rules of grammar. Social studies was not taught until fourth grade. Reading, letter sounds, letter combinations, silent letters, and so on were taught over a span of four years.

Reading in my first grade was all about mastering the basic alphabet sounds and beginning words such as "cat", "mop", "dig", "flag" and "grab". These words can be figured out just by combining the individual letter sounds. This is phonics. Each week we'd learn a couple of sight words as well. Sight words are words that do not follow the rules of phonics. Words such as "said", "who", "the", and "was" are pronounced differently than they look. (The word "was" sounds like "wuz".) Students practice these words so they are recognized on sight.

Building a vocabulary of small words was the start of learning to read, write and spell. Phonics was carried through fourth grade, with various aspects of words learned and the difficulty slowly, but steadily, increased. To me, the way I was taught to read made sense.

Yet here is my non-reading little boy getting four grade levels of information crammed down his throat in a week's time. I feel he was being intellectually damaged by demanding of him to write paragraphs, book reports, identify nouns and verbs, and solve mathematical word problems before he could correctly sound out the word "dog".

Imagine getting your dream job only to find that you are expected to do things you have not been trained to do. Imagine having your boss tell you over and over what a failure you are. Adults would quit the job and move on. Children can't quit school so they just crash and burn.

Damon crashed and he crashed fast. He didn't just think he was stupid, he was convinced he was stupid. Six years of love and support from me, his father, his aunts, uncles and grandparents from both sides of the family went down the drain. At age six, he gave up.

Within two weeks of school starting, I was called in to see the teacher for an urgent meeting. All of my son's academic faults were exposed and discussed right in front of his face. Right in front of his classmates. All the mistakes and errors were listed off one by one.

The teacher did not care that Damon could hear every word. He was not granted the dignity of privacy. No, the teacher pointed out his flaws to my face and in front of his friends.

I was told that Damon confused the letters *b*, *d*, *g*, *p*, and *q*. He confused the numbers 6 and 9. He wrote his name in all capital letters. He would get too embarrassed to read in front of the class when it was his turn. He could not write a proper sentence, paragraph or book report. He did not know the abbreviations of the days of the week. The list went on and on.

I argued that the letters *b*, *d*, *g*, *p*, and *q* looked very similar. If my son confused a "cow" and a "bicycle," I may have been concerned. I was sure that Damon just needed more practice with them.

The teacher continued on her "concerns" saying he confused the numbers 6 and 9. I told her that I'd take Damon off of all check writing and banking responsibilities as a joke.

She did not appreciate my humor.

Practice. Tutoring. Making the alphabet letters in Play-Doh. Taking my son back to simpler work so he had a chance to grasp it, understand it, dare I say "master it" before moving on. These were not an option.

Despite having the ability to speak two languages (clearly demonstrating a capacity to learn) he was about to be diagnosed "learning disabled."

My viewpoint that there was nothing wrong with him and that people need to relax was met with authoritarian contempt.

How silly of me to suggest that my son needed more practice. "Practice" does not help people with learning disabilities. Tutoring will not help someone with ADHD!

How dare I challenge robbing my son of his playtime by giving him three hours of homework each and every night? How naive of me to think that my bilingual son has the capability of learning to read and do math, along with every other school subject. After all, I am not a certified teacher. I am not an "expert."

The only "solution" offered by the teacher was to medicate my son. It was the only hope for kids like him. I asked if the meds would guarantee he would learn to read and the answer was no. The meds would calm him down. (He was already calm so this was not an issue that needed to be addressed.)

"The mind of a child is complex ... and ... we want the best for his future ... and ... the advances in medication ... and ... when can we arrange the evaluation?"

Now I am getting spicy.

Well, how about the teacher wear her actual hat and teach and stop pretending to be a doctor by suggesting medication? I don't go to my dentist to learn to spell and I certainly don't go to a teacher to fill a cavity.

My observations as a mother was that my son was exceptionally bright. He was easy going. He was smart. He could put together LEGO bricks, do jigsaw puzzles, play chess, all without adult direction. I felt Damon was willing and able to learn anything he wanted to.

Further, if Helen Keller could learn (and go on to graduate college), I was 100 percent certain Damon could learn just as well. After all, he did have a major advantage over Helen Keller; Damon could see, hear, and speak.

On a side note, I firmly believe that if Helen Keller was alive today, she'd be prescribed a cocktail of medications. I doubt that there is one educator alive who would think a blind, deaf and mute child could survive without pharmaceuticals. Modern "experts" hiding behind their degrees and big pharma connections would have put Helen on multiple mind-altering medications robbing her of her life, while shaking their heads and stating that this is the best that can be done.

Chances are that Helen's parents would have been medicated as well. If a "certified expert" could not teach my son phonics without suggesting mind-altering medication, then Helen Keller would have had no chance. Period.

The other infuriating aspect to referring to Damon (a normal, healthy little boy) as "handicapped and disabled" is that it serves as a slap in the face to families with children who have actual disabilities. My son is not in the same category as a child with autism, Down syndrome, nor is he non-verbal, deaf, or otherwise challenged with various real mental and physical disabilities.

My son never needed special accommodations. There was nothing wrong with him. Wait. I'll re-word that statement: There was nothing wrong with Damon until he went to school!

Not being able to read does not mean "disabled or handicapped." If I sat in a third-grade class in Russia and could not read what was on the board, I don't think anyone would say I was "mentally handicapped" or "learning disabled."

Not being able to read means not yet able to read. It does not mean "will never be able to read."

In my son's case, the teacher's viewpoint and lesson plans were the problem, not him. My son did not have a "learning disability." His teacher had a "teaching disability."

I did not allow Damon to get evaluated or drugged. But I did not take him out of school either. I was pregnant with my fourth child. I did not think I could manage a newborn, a one-year-old, a three-year-old and homeschooling.

Instead, I ended up working very closely with Damon for the entirety of first grade. I was being a "hands-on mom." I was doing the "right" thing. I made him do his homework before he could play.

Even though I helped him with packets of assignments that were way over his head, I could tell that the connection between my son and I weakened. I could see it in his face. I saw the eagerness to learn, his WANT to learn, diminish.

This affected other areas not directly related to school.

He no longer wanted to be a police officer; he did not care about basketball. He had a subdued attitude about going fishing or having friends sleep over. No matter how much encouragement and cheerleading I did for Damon, at the end of that school year he was convinced he was dumb. He was certain he could not do anything right. He hated school. And I had a front-row seat to view his systematic shutdown.

There is no child on this Earth who should feel this way—special needs or not—no child should feel that they are a useless failure.

Despite my best intentions, I left my son's self-worth in the hands of a system that demonstrated that they could not teach and wanted nothing more than to shut him up with drugs.

I, his mother, the person who is supposed to be his number one advocate, left my son in a so-called "burning building" with a cute lunchbox and backpack hoping that "things would just work out."

I knew that if I did not do something effective, I'd lose my son. He'd lose all faith in my leadership abilities, and he'd end up being one of those unmanageable kids who are disconnected from their families and are smoking pot at age 11.

I had two questions that I was desperate to find the answer to:

When did school start to destroy the child's natural ability to learn, and where the hell was the 1990s version of Anne Sullivan? I really needed to find her.

Part Two

Spoiler alert: In case you have not figured it out, I chose to home-school Damon. I opened my home to include teaching the children of friends. Within a few years, my homeschool activity was so successful I secured the funds needed to move into a storefront at a local strip mall. I will fully cover this journey in later pages.

It wasn't until my homeschool activity became an official private school that I became aware of what was actually happening in mainstream school. Part two of my book is devoted to sharing this information.

Warning to the reader: Part Two is a tough read. It reads almost like a horror story. There is no way around it. It is what it is.

I promise you though that Part Three will give you hope and may even leave you inspired.

Chapter 3

The Takedown of American Education

I attended first grade in 1970 in Cincinnati, Ohio. The school day began at 9:00 a.m. and ended at 3:00 p.m. We had a 30-minute recess before a 45-minute lunch and a 30-minute recess in the afternoon. Recess was not free time. It was organized play. The teacher led and supervised games such as jump rope, duck-duck-goose, and kickball.

We started the day saying the Pledge of Allegiance, with students taking turns holding the flag. We were taught to say, "Good morning," and to address adults as mister, miss, or missus.

The academic part of the day was not stressful. We'd do two pages of handwriting, which consisted of learning to write the alphabet one letter at a time using paper with guidelines. The approach was slow. We'd learn the proper way to write the letter *L* on Monday, then *R* on Tuesday and so on.

Math started with simple patterns and finding similarities and differences in sets or between objects. This led into counting, simple addition and simple subtraction.

Reading started off by learning short vowels, then a few letters, then small words (as in "mat" and "rat") then a few more letters, then a few more small words.

Spelling as its own subject was not part of kindergarten or first grade; grammar and social studies were not introduced as formal subjects until fourth or fifth grade.

Daily lessons were broken up into seat work and doing things at the chalkboard. In between reading, writing and math, we'd sing songs, do crafts, and play classroom games.

I loved first grade. I liked having my own cubby full of school supplies.

Enough Is Enough!

I liked how the teacher changed the classroom decorations each month, I liked seeing my work displayed on the bulletin board. I liked interacting with the volunteer mothers who were on call to help the teacher. It was one of those moms who taught me how the letter *p* was formed by making two different lines. Prior to her coaching, my letter *p* was just an oddly curled line.

My teacher, Mrs. Rudd, was in her early 60s. She had gained cooperation (and respect) from her 25 students without the need to scream or yell.

The first grade I experienced in a Cincinnati public school is not the same as first grade now. My son's first grade in the late '80s was a high-stress, anxiety-inducing nightmare, consisting of five to six hours of seat work during the day and three hours of daily homework at night. No recesses. No breaks. (One would think my son was studying to get a law degree with the pressure he was under.)

So what happened to school?

Why is it that my father's eighth grade skill set from 1942 was much higher than most high school graduates today? How did everyone in my family easily learn to read without therapists, labels and drugs in the '40s, '50s, '60s and '70s, yet in 1991, the educational system deemed my son "unable to learn and in need of a pill" just ten days into the school year?

In 2018, I was a guest speaker at a "concerned citizens" conference. Directly after the event, I was approached by an elderly woman, Ms. Paull, a former English Professor, author, and educational advocate. She was very eager to speak with me, asking for my personal email so she could pass on decades of personal research on the topic of American education. Her only request was that I do something effective with her notes. She made me promise.

One week later Ms. Paull passed away.

In keeping with my promise, I am sharing parts of her research here, particularly pertaining to the subject of reading. I found it rather eye-opening. I think you may feel the same.

A note on religious references: Research into early education methods, particularly for teaching reading, revealed that much of the work that was done was motivated by allowing all people to read the word of God, primarily from the Bible. This trend continued into the early American works regarding education and reading. In this book I am not pushing one religion over another. Every faith had (and has) its own understanding of spirituality and the nature of man. When people were confused in life, or lost their way, they often turned to their faith for guidance, for example by reading from the Bible. However, it is a historical fact that the history of reading, much like the history of America, had religion as its inspiration and foundation.

1534

Martin Luther translated the Catholic Bible from Latin to German, which became an instant bestseller when published. People learned to read so that they could receive the Word of God directly, with the Bible being considered the most important book of this time.

1782

"To suppose that man without language taught himself to speak, seems to me as absurd as it would be to suppose that without legs he could teach himself to walk. Language, therefore, must have been the immediate gift of God." Noah Webster

Following the victory of the Revolutionary War, Noah Webster thought that developing and making firm a language (separate from the King of England) would stabilize America. He published *The American Spelling Book* (most commonly referred to as the *Blue Black Speller*, based on the color of the book cover) which served as a simple guide for spelling and pronouncing words. This speller sold more than 60 million copies and is credited with teaching five generations of Americans to spell and to read.

1784–1785

Noah Webster publishes *A Grammatical Institute of the English Language*, intended as a model to use in American education.

1828

"All the miseries and evils which men suffer from vice, crime, ambition, injustice, oppression, slavery and war, proceed from their despising or neglecting the precepts contained in the Bible." Noah Webster

Perhaps Webster's greatest accomplishment and contribution to mankind was the publishing of the *American Dictionary of the English Language*, which took 28 years to complete. Webster learned 26 different languages for this endeavor. Americans now had an English language that supported the American way of life, which had its foundation primarily in Christian beliefs and not the King of England's ideals. The concept of American patriotism was born, and now through the dictionary the meaning of patriotism could be learned and preserved.

Noah Webster knew then what is true now: knowing the definition of words is key to understanding and maintaining life and liberty. Knowing the definitions of words could put one in agreement with God.

Webster wrote the dictionary to accomplish the following:
- Standardize the American English language,
- Preserve the Christian religion,
- To make the Constitution known,
- To make education a right offered to all,
- To end slavery.

These are sane, pro-survival, high ambitions. Regardless of one's personal religious beliefs, it is clear that Noah Webster intended for America to be a literate, moral, and educated society.

Building upon this major educational achievement, America continued to make advances educationally.

1836

Eclectic Readers, commonly called McGuffey Readers are published. These are a series of reading books intended for first to sixth grades. 120 million copies are sold from 1836 to 1960.

1845

The American Pictorial Primer or the *First Book for Children* is published. This reader starts with the student learning the sounds of individual letters, then letter combinations, then words. The end of the book contains one-page stories and poems.

From an introduction written on a reproduced Primer:

"*The world of the (American Pictorial) Primer is a happy world. At first, birds and animals are prominent, then little children at play, and finally the work and recreation of adults. The cat purrs to 'show her love for you', horses are 'very kind and gentle', and the rooster crows in the morning to let us know when to get up. Children share treats with one another, they 'talk and sing as they move along, and are very happy.' It is the world that adults wished it to be, and hoped for through their children.*" James Thorpe

1863

Felters *Natural Series Primary Arithmetic, Grade Three* (A book from my personal library)

From the note to teacher located at the beginning of the book:

"*There is danger in teaching any of the elementary branches, of falling into the habit of monotony which soon robs both teacher and pupil of nearly all the interest they would otherwise feel in these studies.*"

1865

Following the Civil War and the emancipation of slaves, the Freedmen's Bureau was created to provide assistance to both black and white people who lost everything due to the war. "An Act to establish a Bureau for the Relief of Freedmen and Refugees" was signed into law by President Abraham Lincoln on March 3, 1865.

Under this law, more than 1,000 African-American schools were built and staffed. Most of the major African-American colleges in the US today were founded with assistance of the bureau.

Was education perfect? Far from it, but consider that by the time the 1900s rolled around, America boasted a 97 percent literacy rate in schools. The three percent that could not read or write were children who did not go to school (they worked on family farms). Schools at the time prepared students for reality. For life. Students were not educated to pass tests and enter college. They were educated to be stable, moral, contributing adults who lived by the Word of God.

Civics (the study of rights and duties of being a citizen) was taught. Classroom readers contained stories of American patriots and heroes. The American family was represented as two-parent household. People did not "lose their minds" if the word God was mentioned in school, they embraced God.

Students were not a "one size fits all." They were individuals. For example, a third-grade math book that I personally own from 1913, states that MASTERY of skills is the objective. The author reminds the teacher that each child learns differently and at different speeds. *"If it takes a month to learn the fours (time tables), it takes a month. If it takes a year, it is time well spent."*

Another fourth grade math book from the early 1900s states that the love of numbers is inherent in children and that when properly developed through games and play, it results in quick-thinking future entrepreneurs and leaders who are a value to their family, society and God.

America was "one nation under God" and becoming stronger and better educated. Meanwhile, over in Germany, the field of "psychology" was born.

1875

Wilhelm Wundt establishes the world's first psychological laboratory at Leipzig University in Leipzig, Germany, studying and experimenting on man as a stimulus-response animal, not as a spiritual being with free will.

Wundt became known as the "Father of Modern Psychology," studying and experimenting on the brain and nervous system.

1886 and Beyond

After serving as assistant to Wilhelm Wundt (performing psychological experiments) at Leipzig University, James Cattell (a PhD from Leipzig) was the first American to publish a dissertation on psychology.

A few years later, James Cattell became the President of the American Psychological Association.

James' Contribution to Humanity:

In 1921, James Cattell founded the Psychological Corporation with Edward L. Thorndike and Robert S. Woodworth. The corporation was one of the largest creators and administrators of mental tests. (This corporation changed hands and names but became one of the industry's leaders in mental health screenings.)

In terms of reading, James Cattell theorized that reading words was not done by sounding out letters, but by remembering whole words. "*...the way to teach children how to read would be to show them words and tell them what the words were.*" James Cattell

His research led to the replacement of phonics in American schools, putting "whole-word" learning in its place.

1898

The Father of Progressive Education, John Dewey, became one of the main supporters of the "look and say" method. Dewey was a psychologist who had a dream of transitioning America into a socialist country without ever having to wage a war.

In his 1898 essay "The Primary-Education Fetish," Dewey wrote, "*The plea for the predominance of learning to read in early school life because of the great importance attaching to literature seems to me a perversion.*"

Did he just say what I think he said? That teaching a child to read in primary school is a perversion. Just to be sure, I looked up a few words, which I will share here:
- Progressive: favoring social reform
- Fetish: an excessive or irrational devotion or commitment to a thing

- Plea: a request made in an urgent manner
- Predominance: having more importance than others
- Perversion: having or showing a wrong use, as in a perversion of justice

Yes, the so-called "Father of Education" thought teaching first graders to read was a *perversion*. Putting him in charge of education seems about as intelligent as hiring a fox to guard chickens.

1902

The "sabotage" of American education did not happen overnight. It needed to be financed. Here enters John D. Rockefeller Sr., who in an effort to change his image from "greedy businessman" to "humanitarian" donated one million dollars (equivalent to $33 million in 2022) to create the General Education Board.

1913

I am not going to define the words of every quote but I feel these are worth reviewing as they bring home the terrifying message of the "educational dream" stated below.

- yield: to give up or surrender
- docility: easy to train or manage
- molding: something that influences, determines or directs
- conventions: the way something is usually done
- unhampered: not stopped or prevented
- tradition: customs or beliefs (of a religious nature) that get handed down from generation to generation
- responsive: receiving with interest and enthusiasm
- rural: relating to the country (not the city)
- men of learning: thinkers, geniuses, those who enlighten the world and advance mankind

In 1913, the head of the General Education Board wrote: "*In our dream, we have limitless resources and the people yield themselves with perfect docility to our molding hand. The present educational conventions fade from our minds and, unhampered by tradition, we work our own good will upon a grateful and responsive rural folk. We shall not try to make these people or any of their children into philosophers or men of learning or of science.*"

The Rockefeller family would donate another $180 million towards this cause providing major funding for schools across the United States, making Rockefeller very influential in shaping the schools.

A quote from John D. Rockefeller Sr.: *"I don't want a nation of thinkers. I want a nation of workers."*

From a 2022 article, entitled: "Toward a More Robust Study of Mental Health: Rockefeller Foundation Funding for Psychiatry" by Teresa Iacobelli: *"The development of the field of psychiatry in the United States was largely precipitated by Rockefeller Foundation interest and funding.*

"While the Rockefeller Foundation had funded initiatives in what was then termed the field of "mental hygiene" as early as 1914, the real work in building up the field of psychiatry began in the 1930s."

Rockefeller funded Columbia University to bring psychology from Leipzig University to the United States with the intention to train teachers on the false premise that children are but stimulus-response animals and should be treated or taught as one would train a dog.

John Dewey taught at Columbia University for 25 years, beginning in 1905. Dewey's self-appointed mission was to implement a transition to socialism through a change in the educational system. Through research, Dewey found that the biggest resistance to transition from capitalism to socialism was education, specifically literacy skills. High literacy encourages intellectual independence which produces strong individuals who think and do for themselves.

It was Dewey's analysis of individualism that led him to believe that the "socialized" individual could only be produced by first getting rid of the traditional Christian influences in American schools, eliminating emphasis on language and literacy in the primary grades, and turning the children toward socialized activities and behavior.

He then mapped out a long-range, comprehensive strategy that would reorganize primary education to serve the needs of a socialist country. But he cautioned that, *"Change must come gradually. To force it unduly would compromise its final success by favoring a violent reaction."*

Simply stated, the subject of phonics was removed and whole-word learning put in its place. In keeping with the elimination of literacy, math, language and patriotism, the family dynamic and God were also found to have no value. Subjects like geography and civics were replaced with social studies.

Speaking only about reading, despite the fact that the "whole-word" method did not produce literate children, it was heavily promoted and put into public schools. It was popularized by the *Dick and Jane* readers and was used in classrooms throughout the United States for nearly four decades, creating a decline in literacy across America.

By 1955, the reading problem had become so severe that Rudolf Flesch felt compelled to write a book about it called *Why Johnny Can't Read*. In his book, Flesch referenced a textbook that used to be used to teach phonics. *Reading with Phonics* by Hay Wingo. This successful text was laughed out of existence by the incoming "educational experts" who said it lacked substance or was too simplistic.

Almost 30 years later, Flesch wrote another book titled, *Why Johnny Still Can't Read* reemphasizing the fact that the "look-say" method being taught in schools was still producing illiterate children, advocating the need for American schools to return to phonics.

Nothing changed.

I personally have collected over 400 school textbooks and lessons from the late 1800s to the early 1900s. I do not have a copy of every textbook ever published from 110 years ago, but I have enough to form an objective opinion. There is a definite change in the teaching guidelines contained in these books after Rockefeller and his buddies got involved.

Before Rockefeller funded his psychological agenda, children were expected to master skills, honor God and contribute to their families and community. After Rockefeller introduced psychology to education, children were not taught phonics, academic proficiency was based on test scores (not ability), God was completely removed as a guiding authority, and behavior modification began. Here enters lobotomies, electric shock, and mind-altering medication.

In my opinion, the decline of literacy and the rise of learning disabilities and childhood mental health issues are directly related to these so-called "experts" taking over.

And here we are today with failing schools full of disconnected, medicated children who cannot read or write. We have a society that has abandoned its spiritual side, who are active participants to the "selfie driven me-me-me culture" instead of representing their own religious beliefs by knowing the difference between what is right and what is wrong and having the integrity to act upon it.

Stealing, scamming, having multiple sexual partners and general immorality seem to be the "celebrated norm."

This was no accident. It was created. It was funded.

And the money continues to flow. Psychologists and psychiatrists are now considered the authorities on education. I have spoken to a number of college students working for a teaching degree who say that their classes are more about "mental health" than about properly teaching a subject and managing a classroom.

In 2022, the U. S. Department of Education reported that more than half of Americans between the ages of 16 and 74 read at or below a sixth-grade level. This is 54 percent or roughly 130 million Americans who lack the basic skills of reading, writing and math.

It is one thing to be an actual sixth-grader. However, even with perfect attendance and straight "A's" no one expects much from a 12-year-old. Middle schoolers are not called upon to run businesses, solve the economy or negotiate world peace. We leave the big responsibilities for the grown-ups. This is scary when half of American adults only have an academic skill set that is at or below a sixth-grade level. Lack of literacy affects every aspect of day-to-day life from planning to decision making, problem solving, persistence, hard work, health and success.

To this point there is an entire generation of parents who think it is perfectly normal to have children on some type of medication so they can "focus" at school.

There is an entire generation of teachers who do not know that children used to be educated without the need for labels and drugs.

And there is an entire generation of children, prescribed medication like Prozac at age three, growing up unaware of what it is like to not be medicated.

Speaking just about reading (the most important skill taught in school), the American Psychiatric Association states on their current website: *"An estimated 80% of those with learning disorders have an impairment in reading in particular (commonly referred to as dyslexia)."*

Eighty percent is a huge number of children with learning disorders who also cannot read. Maybe if they could read, they would not have "learning disorders."

What if these same children were taught to read properly using actual phonics, the way it was taught until 1930?

Does anyone think that if suddenly we, as a country, started turning out children who loved to read, the pharmaceutical companies would back off, opting *not* to prescribe ADHD medication, thus forfeiting billions in profits?

It was certified educators and psychologists who destroyed reading by replacing phonics with "whole word reading." More recently, the same type of individuals developed the disaster known as Common Core. These same "experts" have reduced the excitement of day-to-day learning into giving a child weekly packets or placing them in front of a computer to be taught from a screen.

Do you really think the people in charge of American education will do the logical thing and go back to what worked?

No. They. Won't.

Chapter 4

Rating Scales, Screenings, Checklists and Labels

I just combed through a two-inch file of checklists and child screenings that I have collected over the years. It is quite depressing.

Checklists are evaluations filled out by parents, teachers, social workers, psychologists and psychiatrists that itemize observations and behaviors of children.

These checklists can be called a number of things: "Teacher Rating Scale," or "Teacher Observation." The NICHQ Vanderbilt Assessment Scale (National Institute for Children's Health Quality) goes so far as to write "PARENT Informant" or "TEACHER Informant" on the top of said checklist.

Honestly, I find the word "informant" slightly alarming considering an informant is a person who reports information about someone to an organization, agency or higher authority. It is noteworthy that Merriam-Webster lists the word "betrayer" as a synonym. Coincidence? I think not.

The practice of "evaluating children with checklists" by "informants" sounds similar to the protocol used in the Nazi T4 program.

A Short History Lesson

In the years leading up to the Holocaust, madman Adolf Hitler targeted infants and children with various mental and physical disabilities, determining them to be economically burdensome. These children were considered to have a "life unworthy of living."

"Useless eaters," a factual term used at the time, encompassed terminally ill, mentally disabled, low IQ, mentally or physically handicapped or emotionally weak. These children needed more care from society but could not contribute to society, so did not fit within Hitler's ideals of creating the "perfect" race.

Basically, German psychiatrists mandated the extermination of any child deemed "unfit to live." Children born into poverty, who likely would not grow to contribute to Hitler's economy were also sought out as "financial dead weight."

The program was named T4. It stands for "Tiergartenstrasse 4" which is an address in Berlin that acted as headquarters to oversee this operation. Justified under the guise of "science," doctors were given God-like powers to decide if someone in their care was "fit to live" or qualified for "mercy killing," also known as euthanasia.

And how were children located for this program? Through official checklists and forms, filled out by parents, teachers, and medical personnel. In some cases, there were financial benefits to "enrolling" one's child.

At Tiergartenstrasse 4 the medical experts reviewed said forms to decide essentially who lived and who died. Children were not interviewed or examined; their medical records were not reviewed. The decision to admit the child to the hospital was based solely on a checklist of symptoms. Families were not permitted to visit children once admitted.

Special wards were established in health centers exclusively for children. Parents were falsely told that their child would receive excellent care from top physicians in their field, when in reality children were starved, neglected, experimented on (psychiatric drugs, lethal injections, brain operations, etc.), or just outright killed.

The research helped to establish the most "cost-effective death." Children were essentially the guinea pigs of the Holocaust to come.

The children were victims of the chemists and medical experts of the day.

The hospital would then report the child's untimely death, blaming it on pneumonia or whatever "feared disease" was in the news at the time. Death certificates were falsified to forward the lie.

We are talking about the systematic, legal murder of babies and children. That bears repeating—the legal murder of infants and children.

Due to public outcry, Hitler publicly shut down the T4 euthanasia program in 1941. However, it continued covertly until 1945. Over 300,000 children and adults were murdered under T4 (and that is just what was reported).

The practice of diagnosing children using checklists continues today and is considered valid within educational and psychological fields. The data gathered on said child is not questioned or challenged. If the teacher, parent, or psychologist checks off an item, it will be considered fact.

The practice of diagnosing off a checklist is not even remotely "scientific." It is at best, an opinion. What if the parent, teacher, or psychologist doesn't like children? What if they cannot manage children? What if they get irritated by children? What if they abuse children?

This method of scrutinizing a child via items listed is extremely flawed, opening the door to false labels and horrific outcomes. What if the child's problem is not an item on the list?

Further, I find the "philosophy" of diagnosing from checklists to be unfairly one-sided.

One-sided means that all sides are not considered. The most obvious oversight: the child! What does he or she have to say?

If checklists were an actual valid form of diagnosing children (which they aren't), then wouldn't it make sense to provide a checklist for the child to fill out, rating their parent and teacher. Wouldn't "science" request input from the child? In 32+ years I have never seen a child given a checklist to fill out that asks them for their opinion. (I don't know of an instance where a child was even asked for their opinion.) The whole system supports a mentality that the adults' opinions are right and the child's view either doesn't matter or is wrong.

I think having a child rate the adults in their life would be very telling.

Questions such as: On a scale from one to ten, with ten being the highest, how much do you feel your parents love you? How often do your parents read to you? Play board games with you? Spend time with you? Cook with you? How often do your parents encourage you? Say they love you? Hug you? How do your parents discipline you? On a scale from one to ten, how much do you trust your parents?

I think it would be important to ask the child if his or her parents do drugs? Smoke? Watch porn? Use foul language? Is the parent violent? Does the parent break the law?

A similar questionnaire would be given to the child to evaluate their teacher. Does the teacher yell? Only point out mistakes? Call the child names, such as stupid? How does the teacher treat the child? On a scale of one to ten, how do you rate the teacher compared to other teachers? (That would blow a few minds!)

Yes, I would be very interested in a checklist that asked the child to evaluate their parents and teachers. Sadly, it will never happen. I am being a bit sarcastic--I disagree with the whole concept of checklists-- but I do think it would be very beneficial for the child to be given a say in matters concerning his or her life and education.

I think asking the child about his or her quality of sleep would be important. This is not addressed.

Checklists do not ask about the child's diet, which I feel is a gross oversight. How many fruits and vegetables does the child consume daily? How much sugar or caffeine? Does the child eat processed/microwavable/fast food?

Current checklists do not include social skills, manners, contribution, games and personal interests. How many board games does the child play each week with family or friends? Or how many hours is the child kept in front of a device (so that the parent does not have to be bothered)? Checklists do not ask if the child contributes to the household by doing chores; does the family cook and eat dinner together? Does the child have a way to earn money? Has the child ever started a business, even if it is selling lemonade or raking leaves? Does the child have a pet? A bike? LEGO sets? How many books do they read each week, month, year? Do they get ample outside time to climb trees, build forts, explore nature? The labeling process does not ask the child about their short term and long term goals. I think this is important as without knowing the child's plans one cannot align his/her education to achieving his/her goals. The child has to have a reason to learn, a reason to go to school. Checklists do not result in an inspired child. Checklists make "failure" an unchangeable reality that is both enforced and accepted.

The other negative impact of the mental health checklists is the fact that the attitudes and behaviors are looked upon as permanent personality traits when they are not. A five-year-old who is "afraid of making mistakes" (an actual checklist item) may very well outgrow it. A child who is shy may overcome it. In my day, it was called "a phase." He is going through his "why" phase and questions everything; she is going through her "monsters-under-the-bed" phase, and so on. As with any "phase" it goes away.

Weak motor skills, such as "has poor handwriting" (an actual checklist item) can easily be remedied (providing the child has functioning fingers) by teaching the child how to control a pencil. This can be done by getting the child to draw or color.

I met a teenager who at age four was diagnosed with "selective mutism" because he refused to speak to the psychologist doing the evaluation. "Selective Mutism" is a bogus label. When this teen was a four-year-old, he spoke without problem to family and friends, yet refused to speak to the therapist (a stranger) so was placed on medication, which he took until eighth grade.

This boy was taught to "not to talk to strangers" and when he, at age four, chose not to talk to a stranger, he was labeled and prescribed pharmaceuticals because he demonstrated "anti-social tendencies" by not talking to a stranger.

Even at age four, one should have the basic right over their own communication. One decides who they are comfortable with and who they are not, and they act accordingly. I find it unfair to make a life-long diagnosis based on an hour interview between a psychologist and a four-year-old.

Imagine doing checklists on a puppy: Eats shoes—check! Barks for no reason—Check! Doesn't listen—Check!

I am not saying children are dogs or should be treated like dogs. The point is the puppy behaves like a puppy and when properly trained becomes "man's best friend." Children behave like children. They change as they grow. They learn and evolve into (hopefully) well-grounded, intelligent, ethical, contributing adults.

Had someone evaluated me at age four, they'd have found that I was obsessed with the Monkees, liked to draw, hated dresses and was convinced an evil snowman lived in the wall.

As an adult, my musical tastes have expanded, I am a decent artist, and my closet is full of dresses. (I moved to Miami so that handled my snowman problem.)

The point is I grew up and changed; I did not stay the same. When I was a child, I was permitted as a child to be "obsessed" with Davy Jones. I was encouraged to draw, and my parents had protocols in place to keep me safe from the "evil snowman" and the occasional monster under the bed. I baked cookies for Santa and left teeth under my pillow for the Tooth Fairy.

I know of children who were stamped with a label and prescribed pills based on a checklist and a three-minute meeting with a psychiatrist. This should be considered medical malpractice, yet it is done daily by the educational "experts" in charge of our schools and in charge of our children.

Here are some actual items that are used as indications of learning or behavior disorders in children:

BASC-2 Behavior Assessment System for Children ages 12 to 21
Psychcorp product #30035, Copyright 2004 Pearson

Parent Rating (Checklist is filled out by parent)

The ratings are N (never) S (sometimes) O (often) A (almost always)

There are 150 items on this particular list. Examples are:

Item #12. Worries about making mistakes.

Item #13. Uses foul language.

Item #58. Says, "I get nervous during tests" or "Tests make me nervous."

Item #71. Repeats one activity over and over.

Item #118. Is chosen last by other adolescents for games.

Item #144. Is easily annoyed by others.

These items are so general that they apply to humans as a whole. I am easily annoyed by others and I am sure I am equally annoying to others. There are days I am more annoyed and other days I am not annoyed at all. I doubt either of these traits show up in a blood test or brain scan. How can this or any of the checklist items be used as an index of mental illness or learning disabilities and a justification for prescribing pharmaceuticals to children?

Another checklist:

ASEBA Achenbach System of Empirically Based Assessment
Copyright 2001 T. Achenbach

Teacher's Report Form for Ages 6-18.

The form has two pages of fill in the blank questions. On the top of page two the form states:

VIII. Compared to typical pupils of the same age:
1. How hard is he/she working?
2. How appropriately is he/she behaving?
3. How much is he/she learning?
4. How happy is he/she?

The rating options are: Much less/Somewhat less / Slightly less / About average / Slightly more / Somewhat more / Much more

How is comparing one child to another a "standard" for diagnosis? What is the scientific definition of a "typical student?"

Back in 1991, was my son "typical?" Did I want him to be "typical?" He was six years old and bilingual. Does this mean his six-year-old classmates who only spoke one language were somehow "not typical"?

How can we determine how "hard" someone works compared to someone else of the same age? When I was six years old, I was a straight "A" student and did not work "hard" at all. Where does this fit in? I do not think it would be fair to rate my ability as it compares to someone else. Or to rate another's ability compared to me.

I have four children. All raised the same. Yet, at age five, all four were drastically different. They moved at different speeds, they had their own likes and dislikes, their responses to life were different. It would be grossly unfair to "compare" them to each other.

I think there should be a clearly defined "standard." For example, one kindergarten standard would be "student can count to 20." The comparison of said standard would not be with other students, the comparison would be to the student himself or herself. If it takes the student five minutes to learn to count to 20, that is great. If it takes five months, that is fine, too. Progress is being made. Plus the child is only five years old. Maybe he or she just needs more time. People seriously need to relax. No one can predict what changes a child will go through as they grow up. I've seen children happily spend two and a half years doing first grade work then suddenly "click," ending up a year or so ahead.

Here are my other problems with checklists:

#1 - The checklists list normal childhood behaviors and turn them into indications of mental illness.

#2 - The checklists are based on opinion (not science). What if the person giving their opinion is an idiot?

If we are really going to help the child then we have to be interested enough to speak *to* the child, not *at* the child, and get his or her viewpoint.

The word "to" in this sense means the communication actually arrives.

And if the parent and teacher "must" evaluate a child from a checklist with 155 items listed, then to be fair, and to get an accurate assessment, the child should be given a similar checklist to rate the adults in his or her life.

2023-24 Private School or Educational Contact Request for Additional Information

The above is the name of an official online evaluation form used by Miami-Dade County Public Schools. I was asked to fill the form out on a previous student so that the new school "*Could better understand the concerns and needs of student....*"

The form requested information about the student, such as name, birthdate, grade level, test scores, and report card grades. There is a section asking about recent evaluations and educational plans.

Question #18 - "*In what areas is the student currently experiencing concerns?*" Five options are listed to check: reading/writing, science, mathematics, social-emotional, communication. The computer program allows all five options to be checked. This is in contrast to questions 11, 12, 13, 14 and 32, which all ask about the student's strengths in various skills, but the computer only permits one box to be checked.

In other words, the way the form has been created allows the student to exhibit all concerns listed, but for any question pertaining to the student's strength or ability, he or she is only permitted to have one box checked per question.

This goes beyond being a one-sided form; it is incredibly unfair.

Kayden

Kayden was raised by his grandmother in another state. The labeling procedure started on September 13, 1994. This date is significant as it was only Kayden's second week of kindergarten. He was five.

The teacher filled out a form titled:

EIP (Early Intervention Program) CHECKLIST FOR KINDERGARTEN ELIGIBILITY

The checklist contained 11 items based on QCC (Quality Core Curriculum) content standards.

The teacher checked the following characteristics:

- Difficulty identifying upper- and lower-case letters of the alphabet out of sequence.
- Unable to recognize and select numerals for 0 through 10.
- Demonstrates difficulty in identifying basic geometric shapes: rectangle, oval and diamond.
- Demonstrates difficulty cutting on a straight line with scissors.
- Demonstrates difficulty in recalling first and last name.
- Demonstrates difficulty printing name. (He wrote the first letter of his name backwards.)
- Demonstrates difficulty following directions.

A student would have to meet at least six of the stated characteristics to qualify for an Early Intervention Program. Kayden met seven out of eleven points. Kindergarten had just started and this little boy was being targeted just two weeks into the school year.

He was essentially expected to have kindergarten skills before actually completing kindergarten.

The teacher also noted that Kayden's drawings were "immature in nature."

The Octopus versus Spiderman, by Kayden

I am not shocked that his art looks the way it does. I am stunned that an adult with a degree would expect anything but "immature art" from a person who is only five.

The teacher could have used "The Octopus versus Spiderman" to inspire Kayden to create his own comic strips, which would have required him to draw more, write more and get creative. His formation of letters may have improved.

But no. We need to make sure he knows he is inept. We need to tell his grandmother just how incapable he is. If he cannot count to ten by the second week of school, "science" tells us he will never be able to balance a checkbook so is doomed to a life of failure.

And of course, little five-year-old Kayden was put on a cocktail of medications (Strattera and Adderall to start with). As he got older, more medications were prescribed.

There is no mention of *why* the grandmother was raising him. No mention of the parents being alive, dead, in jail, or where they were. I think this information is important. The age of the grandmother was also omitted. Was she 49 or 99? This would make a big difference in raising this boy, or any five-year-old for that matter. A young grandparent may have more tolerance for an active child. An older grandparent may consider their grandchild "hyper-active" when, in fact, the child is just being five.

Either way, at age five, Kayden was placed in an Early Intervention Program and prescribed medications based on a checklist listing 11 things.

Simone

When Simone arrived to start ninth grade, her psych report was over an inch thick and dated back to the age of seven. Due to a family situation, Simone was placed in foster care. As a foster child, Simone was subjected to mental health screenings, which were required from her teachers as well as the social worker assigned to her case.

The psych evaluation determined that Simone was of average intelligence for a seven-year-old, with exceptional communication skills. However, her teacher reported that Simone had trouble staying focused and sometimes struggled with reading and math. In addition to the screening performed by the teacher, Simone's mother was asked to fill out a checklist on her daughter. The mother reported Simone to be "below average" in doing dishes, cleaning her room and sweeping the floor. (Simone was seven!)

From the **Learning Disabilities Diagnostic Inventory**: "*No longer must diagnoses of Learning Disabilities be dependent solely upon IQ tests, Achievement tests.... Learning Disability Diagnostic Inventory* [a fancy name for a checklist or screening] *provides a way to reintroduce clinical/teacher judgment back into the diagnostic process.*"

In other words, there is no need for scientific tests, we can diagnose a child from the judgment of a teacher and parent, and it only takes ten minutes to label a child.

In addition to Simone being diagnosed via a 15-item checklist, she was directly observed by a psychologist, who followed her around school part of the day. In the psych report it is stated: None of the other students seemed to be distracted by the novelty of my presence, but that was a distraction for Simone who did not know that I was observing (specifically) her.

I think I would be curious if some random stranger showed up in my classroom. The fact that other children did not question this person's presence really doesn't matter. Maybe Simone was the most aware student in her class and the only one who noticed. The fact that Simone seemed alert to a "nearby stranger" was turned into a red flag (as if "normal" children should not give a second look to a lingering stranger).

The psych in this instance wrote a detailed four-page report, noting every time a seven-year-old Simone flipped her hair, stepped out of the line going from class to class, adjusted her dress or looked out the window.

An academic test found Simone to be "behind" in reading, writing and math, which again, could be the fault of the useless textbooks and lesson plans used in school.

The report states that her "ability score" (aptitude) is far higher than her "academic skills."

Missing from the case file were the circumstances that resulted in Simone being placed in foster care. She was away from her mother for almost a year. I do not know the circumstances, but I would guess that the mother got into some type of trouble or was unstable. (I honestly understand that things do happen.) That said, why would the mother be asked to fill out a rating scale and why would that rating scale not be questioned?

Between the rating scales of the mother and teacher, and the observation report written by the psychologist following her for half a school day, it was determined that seven-year-old Simone was learning disabled and in need of medication, which she took until she was 13. At one point she was on three different pills.

Chapter 5

The Chemical Alteration of the Central Nervous System

I am not "anti-doctor." I am not "anti-medicine." Open-heart surgery saved my life at age three. If it weren't for modern medicine, I would not even be here. Much later, an emergency C-Section saved my daughter's life. I am very thankful for advances in medicine.

That said, I do have an issue with children as young as three being falsely labeled and put on mind-altering medication.

CNS stands for Central Nervous System. CNS medication directly affects and alters the central nervous system.

Adderall, Ritalin, Focolin, Strattera and Vyvanse are a few of the CNS medications used to treat ADD/ADHD.

This is what a Google search states about CNS medication: "*Central Nervous System (CNS) depressants are medicines that include sedatives, tranquilizers, and hypnotics. These drugs can slow brain activity, making them useful for treating anxiety, panic, acute stress reactions, and sleep disorders.*" Mar 6, 2018

My son's teacher recommended that my son's central nervous system be chemically altered as a "solution" to his difficulties learning to read. An educator (not a doctor) said, with full authority, that my son needed CNS medication so he could successfully determine the differences between letters and numbers.

This was a lie.

There is no drug on the market that would get my son to learn the alphabet.

Further, altering my six-year-old son's "central nervous system" before his baby teeth had fallen out, while his young brain was growing, could, according to the listed side-effects, impair him, kill him or permanently disable him.

Oh, and by the way, the drugs may make him want to commit homicide or suicide or both.

Why on earth would I essentially poison my son, potentially ruin his brain function, potentially drive him to suicide, on the advice of a teacher because he confused numbers and letters? Makes. No. Sense.

Personally, I think a fully functioning central nervous system is essential for the learning process.

Fact: Adderall prescriptions are listed (per a Google search) as the most prescribed to address ADHD.

Side effects: weight loss, heart attack/failure, hallucinations, aggression, hostility, suicidal/homicidal thoughts, or actions.

Further, I find the term "side-effect" grossly misleading. A "sunburn" is not a side-effect to "sun exposure." A sunburn is a primary effect to sun exposure.

Insomnia, weight gain, weight loss, stunted growth, heart failure, suicidal/homicidal thoughts are just a few of the "side-effects" (primary effects) listed for ADHD medication.

This begs to ask: Would my child suffer insomnia, weight gain, weight loss, stunted growth, suicidal or homicidal thoughts if he were educated the way I was back in the late '60s?

This is taken directly from Drugs.com about Adderall:

Adderall may be habit-forming, and this medicine is a drug of abuse.

Stimulants have caused stroke, heart attack, and sudden death in people with high blood pressure, heart disease, or a heart defect.

Adderall may cause new or worsening psychosis (unusual thoughts or behavior), especially if you have a history of depression, mental illness, or bipolar disorder.

You may have blood circulation problems that can cause numbness, pain, or discoloration in your fingers or toes.

Call your doctor right away if you have: signs of heart problems—chest pain, feeling light-headed or short of breath; signs of psychosis—paranoia, aggression, new behavior problems.

Adderall Side Effects

Get emergency medical help if you have signs of an allergic reaction to Adderall: hives; difficulty breathing; swelling of your face, lips, tongue, or throat.

Call your doctor at once if you have:
- *signs of heart problems - chest pain, trouble breathing, feeling like you might pass out;*
- *signs of psychosis - hallucinations (seeing or hearing things that are not real), new behavior problems, aggression, hostility, paranoia;*
- *signs of circulation problems—numbness, pain, cold feeling, unexplained wounds, or skin color changes (pale, red, or blue appearance) in your fingers or toes;*
- *a seizure (convulsions);*
- *muscle twitches (tics); or*
- *changes in your vision.*

Seek medical attention right away if you have symptoms of serotonin syndrome, such as: agitation, hallucinations, fever, sweating, shivering, fast heart rate, muscle stiffness, twitching, loss of coordination, nausea, vomiting, or diarrhea.

Adderall can affect growth in children. Tell your doctor if your child is not growing at a normal rate while using this medicine.

Common Adderall side effects may include:
- *stomach pain, loss of appetite;*
- *weight loss;*
- *mood changes, feeling nervous;*
- *fast heart rate;*
- *headache, dizziness;*
- *sleep problems (insomnia); or*
- *dry mouth.*

This is not a complete list of side effects and others may occur. Call your doctor for medical advice about side effects. You may report side effects to FDA at 1-800-FDA-1088.

Geez. I wonder what the COMPLETE list of side-effects looks like.

I have had the unfortunate opportunity to speak to three different mothers who lost a teenager due to the effects of the ADHD medications they were taking. Two fourteen-year-old boys suffered heart failure, the other teenager, a girl, took her own life. These children were placed on CNS meds in *kindergarten*. None made it to high school. It is my opinion that teenage heart failure and suicide are not normal.

From an article: Prescribing Adolescents Multiple Psychiatric Drugs Now the Norm: *In 2020, the journal Pediatrics (https://publications. aap.org/pediatrics/article/146/1/e20192832/77028/Attention-Deficit-Hyperactivity-Disorder-and) reported that 40.7 percent of people ages 2 to 24 who were prescribed a drug for attention deficit hyperactivity disorder also were prescribed at least one other medication for depression, anxiety, or another mood or behavioral disorder.*

Further, researchers found more than 50 psychotropic medicines prescribed in such combinations.

In a short search, I found dozens of similarly named articles reporting children being prescribed multiple medications at an alarming rate.

In my opinion, any deaths or life-threatening health issues linked to CNS medications should result in lawsuits against the doctor prescribing the drugs and the company manufacturing them.

Children on multiple meds is not good. I personally have never met a medicated child who is stable, independent, contributing and happy. I personally find the longer the child is on ADHD medication, the harder it is to teach them or get them to make progress.

My advice (to take or leave) is if you are told to medicate your child due to academic problems, ask how many cases the medication has cured. Then ask, if the medication ends up harming your child, who do you sue. I feel these are fair questions.

I am very fortunate that I chose not to medicate my son. My heart goes out to families who decided to try the meds and ended up regretting it.

Finally, if Helen Keller were alive today, being a blind, deaf and mute six-year-old, how many medications do you think she'd be prescribed? Do you think the drugs would result in her learning to communicate, read, write, and become a contributing member of society?

I know the answer. And so do you.

Human Lab Rats

In 2007 or 2008, two 20-something individuals showed up at my school during afternoon classes in slick business attire and a rolling briefcase. They were in the area and asked for a meeting with me, the principal. They were drug reps for an ADHD medication that had not yet gone on the market.

The reps explained that they were working off a list of local daycares, public, private and charter schools, and all after-school organizations to find children to enroll in a drug study. The study was being conducted through a local university. They explained that before a medication goes public, it must pass rigorous and strict drug study guidelines. The said medication must be tested in clinical trials, involving children of all ages. They came to my school wanting to drug my students. The more kids, the better.

(Despite my instant mental rejection of these two people, I smiled and listened to what they had to say.)

The reps explained that this particular study offered three levels of participation, each with financial compensation for my personal participation. Funds would be issued in the form of a check and could be made out to me personally (as I am the owner of the school) or the funds could be made out in the name of the school.

(I cannot believe what I am hearing, but please tell me more.)

The first level of participation would involve me submitting the contact information of my past, present and future students. I could include the contacts of family and friends, even if they did not have children. I could provide the addresses of people I send Christmas cards to; it was the quantity of names that was important. Each address would be put into a database and contacted independently. For every name, address and phone number submitted, I would receive $100.

The second level of participation required that I complete a Student Rating Checklist (a list of 35 items, rating characteristics on a "never, sometimes, often" basis). For each completed checklist, I or the school would receive $500. It was made clear that I did not have to interview children. The Student Rating was only based on *observation*.

The third level of participation would require the most commitment. After completing a checklist, I would sit with the parent/guardian of said child and discuss the importance of the drug trial.

For every child that I got to take the meds, I'd get paid $5,000.

$5,000 for each child on meds. This was potentially $260,000 for the 52 kids I had enrolled at the time.

(What in the hell was this about? $5,000 kick-back per child!)

I voiced that I had no interest in participating in the drug study as I considered experimenting on children to be a crime.

The male rep started shaking his head in disbelief. He told me that out of hundreds of daycares, private, public, charter, Catholic, Baptist, and after school sports programs I was the only one in South Florida to refuse the money.

The female representative, looking like she just stepped off the set of a Hallmark movie added, "*And let's face it, Barbara. Your school is small and ugly. Think of what you could do with the funding.*"

So, I responded to these snakes.

"Well, let's face it. If I want to fund my school with drug money, I'll just go find a cocaine dealer. This is Miami, after all. And the coke dealer won't push his cocaine on children, which means he has higher morals than you two."

I did not stop there. As I have mentioned, my school is basically a one room schoolhouse located in a former karate studio at a mall. My office is right in the middle, with glass windows that allow unobstructed views. If I could reach through the glass from my desk, I could touch a high school student. That's how small my space is.

I handed these morons a three-page list of side-effects associated with current ADHD medications and pointed out specific high school kids who had horror stories related to the medication they were prescribed years prior. "That boy has a facial tick. That one attempted suicide when he was ten. That one has permanent liver damage associated with years of Ritalin use. That one has an irregular heartbeat," and so on.

There was only one high school student who had never been labeled or medicated and that was my youngest son, who was 16 at the time.

The reps looked a little shocked but still had smug, know-it-all looks on their faces. Clearly, these two were not getting it.

I excused myself to address the high school class. I told them that the suits in my office just offered me $260,000. The kids were ecstatic! We could get a new building! We could build a basketball court! We could have dances!

I told them there was a catch. In order to receive the funds each student would have to take a new psychiatric medication for ADHD as the "experts" know you all can't learn without taking mind-altering drugs.

The room turned hostile in a blink. Teenagers stood up, hands on hips, nostrils flaring, eyes on fire. The kids could not believe this was happening right in front of their faces. The drug reps were listening in to everything I said.

I addressed my high schoolers sincerely, yet firmly. I think it is best to just relay this "mini-speech" word-for-word.

"No one can get hurt. Look at me. No one gets hurt. The anger that you are feeling right now is completely justified. These people just offered me money in exchange for your health and future. Anger is correct. Hold on to it but don't do something dumb. Violence is not the goal here. I am going to deliver some much-needed reality. But no one gets hurt. Got it?

Good. Listen closely."

I walked back into my office, where I remained standing, telling the drug reps that they should do something positive with their college degrees instead of damaging the minds and bodies of children.

I asked them to look in the eyes of each and every high schooler. I wanted them to see the lives they were trading for commissions. I said, and I quote: "*I suggest you pack up your brochures, take back the checklists, and get the hell out of my office because I am dismissing high school early and they may kick your ass in the parking lot. Class dismissed!*"

The reps literally ran from the building followed by 14 angry teenagers. No one got hurt. No punches were thrown. The kids were back in their seats within three minutes. But the kids let them have it. In under three minutes, I heard shouts of, "*I have to see a heart doctor every six months because of you!*" "*I wanted to kill myself when I was seven!*" and so on.

Upon returning to class, one young man, a 14-year-old with a history of taking up to six medications at once, said: "*Miss! I used the 'F' word. I am okay if I get punished.*"

He was not reprimanded for foul language because sometimes the "F" word is appropriate, especially when lives are on the line.

Santiago

Santiago started ADHD medication when he was four. His parents thought this would help him do better in school. The meds did not help him because there is not a pill or combination of pills that raises literacy levels.

Santiago continued to struggle academically which affected his self-esteem. By the time he was ten, he was prescribed anti-depressants to take with the ADHD meds. When he started having trouble sleeping, he was given yet another drug.

By the time Santiago was 14, he was on multiple psychotropics and nearly catatonic. He was pale. He looked undernourished. He kept to himself. The parents thought this was "normal teenage behavior."

After all, Santiago had always kept to himself. (In reality, Santiago had always been drugged.)

There was a barbecue that my youngest boys (Santiago's age) attended. My boys were climbing palm trees to retrieve coconuts, they were catching bait fish, they were doing back flips off a boat, eating full meals every fifteen minutes, and doing all the things teenage boys do at a picnic near the ocean.

Meanwhile, Santiago remained seated at a shaded picnic table, staring at the ground. He did not talk, he did not eat and he did not engage. My boys invited him to swim or fish and he just declined with a weak smile or slight shake of his head. One wonders if he even knew a picnic was going on.

A woman at the picnic, Santiago's aunt, told me: *"Barbie, it was so sad. Beautiful day, but he did not move. He just sat there. All day he just stayed in one spot."*

Two weeks later, Santiago's parents were in my office at school, with a translator, asking for my help with their son. They had already requested the pediatrician get their son off all of the meds because they saw for themselves how "lively" my boys behaved without medication, in contrast to their son. They were devastated they did not see this earlier.

I agreed to enroll Santiago in the ninth grade, making no guarantees that he would earn a high school diploma. On a TerraNova test of basic skills, he scored at a first or second-grade level in reading, language and math.

(TerraNova tests are standardized achievement tests widely used in the United States to assess students' academic knowledge and skills in subjects such as reading, mathematics, and science from kindergarten through 12th grade, serving educational purposes such as student placement, accountability, and tailored instruction.)

Santiago could not do basic addition or subtraction. He could not write a complete sentence. He did not use punctuation or capitalization, and his handwriting was impossible to read, yet his public school kept passing him.

One would think if ADHD medicine worked, he'd be closer to grade level.

The thing that all the teachers, experts, therapists and doctors missed was that *Santiago did not understand English!* His parents only spoke Spanish at home. He was given quizzes and tests in a language he did not understand. He did not respond to the teacher because he did not understand her. No wonder he struggled. This boy was drugged because of a language barrier. Even at 14, he was not fluent in English, yet he was expected to read English literature and write book reports with passing grammar.

Instead of enrolling him in English as a Second Language classes when he was four, Santiago was placed on a cocktail of drugs.

How many "certified experts" consulted the family over the years? How many therapists? How many tests, checklists and observations missed something I, a person with no degree or formal training, found in two minutes of speaking with him and his parents? It is kind of infuriating to think what this boy was subjected to over the years.

It took Santiago five years to earn a standard high school diploma. Slow and steady—he made it. While that is good news, I believe the medication permanently impaired him as he never quite came out of his "fog."

Nina

Nina was a 14-year-old ninth grader referred to my school by a child psychologist who was working with her family. The psychologist felt Nina would do better in a smaller school setting as she struggled in school, which was affecting her self-esteem.

She did do better.

The psychologist was happy that in just a few months Nina was doing her work, made a few friends and even took the lead in a Christmas show. And was fantastic! The girl was fearless in front of the audience. She was funny, animated, and received a well-deserved standing ovation at the end.

However, part of the family therapy required that the mother fill out a Parent Rating checklist on her daughter. Nina's mother said her daughter was rude, that she'd stay hours in her room, she ignored her mother, did not want to do chores.

Per the mother, Nina was "obsessed" with drawing. She took her sketchbook everywhere. She drew in the car, she drew at the dinner table, she drew when she was supposed to be sleeping. Often, Nina drew at lunchtime at school. Nina showed me her sketchbook. It was full of hearts, unicorns, vampires, rainbows, kittens and flowers.

Shortly after the "Parent Rating" checklist was completed, Nina was put under the care of a psychiatrist.

Based on the parent rating checklist (and on the checklist alone) the psychiatrist found Nina suffered from Obsessive-Compulsive Disorder. Nina told me herself that the psychiatrist only spoke to her for a few minutes when getting diagnosed. (A fact verified by the family therapist.)

The psychiatrist prescribed this girl Zoloft to "treat" her drawing obsession!

On what planet is "art" considered a "mental illness"? What harm is the girl doing? What if she is the next Picasso or Rembrandt? Why the hell are we drugging her? The girl is not roaming the streets, doing drugs, or meeting online predators. Her mother should be supporting her sketching activity, not condemning it. Why on earth is "drawing" now a sign of a mental disorder?

I was alerted by the family psychologist that Nina was prescribed medication and that it would be appreciated if I could monitor her for side-effects or changes in behavior. I refused as I am not qualified to recognize side-effects to medication. The psychologist became fed up with me for my "attitude" as I was not "cooperating" with the care of the girl.

Family Psychologist: *"Well, what would you do?"*

My answer: *"I'd enroll Nina in after-school art classes. She has talent. She needs instruction, not drugs."*

This was a lightbulb moment for the psychologist, who felt this was an excellent idea.

Art classes were suggested to the mother, but firmly turned down. The psychiatrist knew best. He said the girl needed Zoloft for her "obsession" so Zoloft she got.

I cannot help but wonder what would have happened if this girl grew up encouraged to draw. What if her mother framed her art and turned it into gifts, or paid her to make family Christmas cards? What if Nina felt that she was valued and appreciated as an artist and not a problem?

Well, Nina continued the Zoloft. Within a few months she no longer wanted to draw—she no longer did her schoolwork, she no longer participated in class. The family therapist suggested she go back to public school as she seemed "well adjusted."

She was not "well adjusted." She was a zombie. The "experts" nullified this vibrant, creative spirit with mind-altering drugs.

Note: If your child is on ADHD medication and you wish to exercise your parental rights to stop treatment, it is very important you seek a qualified medical doctor for professional guidance. Abruptly discontinuing these (or any) drugs can be dangerous and should be closely monitored under the care of a qualified physician.

Chapter 6

The IEP and Low Expectations

An IEP is, in Florida, called an Individualized Educational Plan. These may be called different names in different states, but the purpose is the same:

The IEP is a document that is designed to meet your child's unique educational needs. It's not a contract, but it does guarantee the necessary supports and services that are agreed upon and written for your child.

Source: Florida Department of Heath

An IEP is issued after checklists and various evaluations are complete. An IEP has two stated purposes:

1. To establish measurable annual goals for the child;
2. To state the special education, related services, supplementary aids and services that the public agency will provide to, or on behalf of, the child.

"To qualify for an IEP, children as young as 3 years of age, up until 12th grade in high school, must have a physical or mental impairment that limits at least one major activity, such as reading. The impairment must be permanent and not a temporary disability, such as a broken leg." Source Google Search: Miami-Dade IEP Purpose

IEPs are authored by a team of people. There are several points to the above information worth looking into. However one stands out: **The impairment must be permanent**.

The NICHD (National Institute of Child Health and Human Development), considered an authority on diagnosing learning disabilities, states on their website: *"Learning disabilities have no cure, but early intervention can lessen their effects."* Source: Nichd.nih.gov

The NICHD logo can be found on many of the mental health/student screenings forms. But I digress.

I never once thought my son's confusion of the letters "b and d" to be a *permanent* condition. I had 100 percent certainty that my son possessed the full ability to recognize letters and numbers. I believed he had the full capacity to read.

At age three, my youngest son walked around with underwear on his head. I was pretty confident that this was not a permanent condition and that by the time he graduated high school this would no longer be his choice of fashion.

The only individuals who thought Damon had a "permanent mental/learning disability" were the certified educators and psychologists. And these so-called "experts" wanted to drug my son just ten days into the school year.

Just because Damon did not know the alphabet, did not mean he could not learn the alphabet. (Starbucks gives new employees a full three months to learn the ropes—my son was given less than ten days to master letters and numbers.)

I have personally viewed over one hundred IEPs for students of various ages, grades, races and so on. The student's name, age, grade are reported. The name and date of tests, evaluations, and other information are noted. Special accommodations, such as sitting closer to the board or having extended time to take academic tests, are included. Medications are listed. Everything looks very legit.

Then one takes a closer look.

IEPs include a section titled **"The Measurable Goal."** This is the "experts' solution and expectations" for dealing with the child, and the best way to accommodate said learning disabilities. This is the meat of the individualized program and is based on years of college, many degrees, and hours of observation/evaluations of the child.

Here are exact **Measurable Goals** from various IEPs:

Female Student: Age 10

Medication: Prozac 30 mg; along with two other medications to treat high blood pressure and nausea

Measurable Goal: XXXXX will solve grade level word problems that involve two or three steps, by gathering the information she needs to solve the problems, using circling, boxing and underlining, and solve the problems with 70% accuracy, given three out of four opportunities.

Aside from the fact a 10-year-old is taking Prozac along with two other anti-depressants, the experts feel that doing math with a 70 percent accuracy is a valid goal. And then she only has to do that three out of four times.

I would almost understand if a teacher moved to label a child if the best the child could do was grasp 70 percent of the material. I could almost think with that.

But to have 70 percent accuracy as the goal—and only expect it to be attained 75 percent of the time—is not only incredibly stupid, but it also does a grave injustice to the child.

Further, the Evaluation Procedure consists of the teacher "observing the girl and grading her work every week." I thought that teachers were supposed to "observe students and grade their work" as part of their day-to-day job. But what do I know? I do not have a PhD.

Enough Is Enough!

From another Individual Educational Plan:

Male Student: Age 14

Medication: Adderall 30mg

Special Accommodations: Ignore minor inappropriate behaviors/Do not penalize for poor handwriting/motor skills

In my opinion, this was a normal boy. He was four grade levels behind because he was not made to take any responsibility for his part in his education. In my opinion, this boy had no issues with motor skills. In fact, his parents said he was a "gamer" and spent hours using various devices. His fingers obviously worked, yet his handwriting was impossible to read.

In terms of behavior he was, for lack of a better word, a jerk and appeared to have no clue how to behave in social situations. He was never corrected by his parents. He made fun of others, interrupted the class, made hurtful, inappropriate comments, all "verified" in his IEP. Clear "evidence" that he suffered from various behavioral disorders.

Day one at my school he was required to re-do all assignments that were sloppy. In math, if the problem could not be easily read by the teacher, it was marked wrong. His "minor inappropriate behaviors" were not tolerated. This was not accomplished with a "heavy fist." It was presented as a reasonable request. I asked him how many times could a video game malfunction before he'd get frustrated. He responded three times. I explained that the teacher is trying to run a class and that HE is acting like a broken video game, which is frustrating. And as I only had one eighth grade class, if the teacher decided she could not work with the constant interruptions, he would be dismissed. I think this was fair.

In just three months using this approach, he was a different kid at school. He was proud of his work, was making progress in math. His behavior improved, though he remained on my "radar." He started helping to organize bookshelves and take out trash. He made a point to say "good morning" when he arrived to school, and he stopped by my office to say "goodbye" before leaving.

Unfortunately, his parents and psychologist disagreed with my approach. They found him to be nothing but a problem: at home he had to be asked several times to do chores and he often used bad language. (Sounds like a teenager to me.) While the parents could not deny their son was improving academically, they felt he would do better with more meds at a military-style boarding school for juvenile delinquents. Last I heard, he ran away.

The following are more examples of statements and comments taken from IEPs of students I have worked with:

Male Student: Age 13

Medication: Adderall, Zoloft, Stattera to address ADHD and Bi-Polar Disorder

Annual Measurable Goal: When faced with a situation, XXXXX will use personal skills to solve problems, without adult intervention except when necessary 75% of the time.

During structured and less structured settings, XXXXX will refrain from verbal gestures that may reinforce or escalate an existing conflict between peers with 75% accuracy.

How could any of the above be monitored? What if this boy had six months of "good behavior" but suddenly decided to harass or harm your child? Should we ignore it? According to the "experts," this boy acting out 25 percent of the time is considered acceptable. It is progress, according to the experts. What if one of the times his behavior was "ignored" he caused real harm to another human being?

⋅ § ⋅

Male Student: Age 12

Medication: None listed.

Annual Measurable Goal: During teacher instruction, XXXXX will focus 80% of the time.

Again, how will this be enforced or monitored? Are the experts really saying that daydreaming 20 percent of the time is an acceptable goal? Maybe the IEP specialists should be a passenger in a car where the driver is only expected to focus 80 percent of the time.

⋅ § ⋅

Male Student: Age 12

Measurable Goal: XXXXX will be able to use math concepts to solve problems with number sense, concepts, and operations according to the Sunshine State Standards with 70% accuracy, using real word problems.

Once again, educational experts lose all credibility by thinking 70 percent accuracy is acceptable in math. It just isn't.

⋅ § ⋅

Female Student: Age 9

Medication: Yes. For borderline ADHD.

Annual Measurable Goal: Student will solve two step word problems involving whole numbers, fractions, decimals and percents using the basic 4 operations with 75% accuracy as measured by graded work samples.

There were seven people involved with this girl's IEP, including both parents. The IEP folder I received on this student was over an inch thick. She was given Measurable Goals of achieving 70 to 80 percent accuracy in reading, writing, math, language—basically all subjects.

The IEP reported that this girl excelled in reading and math. However, her classroom performance "is impacted by deficits in auditory processing and weakness in verbal ability." That's just a bunch of vocabulary words that mean the girl was shy and got nervous speaking in front of the class. Experts determined that she qualified as "speech impaired" and Specific Learning Disabled.

From the American Psychiatric Association's website: "*Specific learning disorders are neurodevelopmental disorders that are typically diagnosed in early school-aged children, although may not be recognized until adulthood. They are characterized by a persistent impairment in at least one of three major areas: reading, written expression, and/or math.*"

According to the child's IEP she excelled at reading and math; written expression was not mentioned as an issue, so labeling and drugging her makes no sense. She did not fit the psychiatric definition of "specific learning disorders."

One evaluation found her to be "aggressive and hostile," another listed her as "hearing impaired." Both statements were outright lies. This girl was about as aggressive as Betty White at church on Sunday. Her hearing was fine. At age ten, she was nervous to read in front of her classmates. Period.

On a side note, this girl excelled in my school. She gained confidence and, when in high school, wore a fedora while lip-synching and dancing to a Frank Sinatra song in front of 40 teenagers. She did not need drugs. She needed to be permitted to grow up.

Another child's IEP listed "verbal encouragement" under Special Accommodations to address their learning disabilities. Do we really need a group of PhDs to say a child should get "verbal encouragement" as part of their education? Does encouragement, love and respect really fall under "special accommodation?"

I argue that children do so much better when they feel supported.

Children should feel they are liked by their teacher. This applies to all children. It actually applies to humans in general.

I could write from literally hundreds of IEPs that I have personally read. The Measurable Goal from one IEP to the next is nearly the same: a C-, mediocre student. That is the best the educators and psychologists can hope for. They don't even guarantee your child will understand anything, but let's make the goal 70 to 75 percent accuracy. Oh, and let's drug them while we're at it.

That's what America needs. A generation of drug dependent, C- performers. Here is the deliberate "dumbing down" of our children in writing.

How about we round up all the people on the IEP panel and demand they settle for haircuts that are 70 percent accurate, by barbers who only focus 80 percent of the time. Maybe our IEP panel of experts would be happy to go to a restaurant and receive a meal with 70 percent accuracy. How about car repairs, banking, kitchen remodels, veterinarian services? Better yet, how about a marriage partner who is faithful 75 percent of the time!

If a waiter consistently served meals that were only 70 percent accurate, or a cake decorator continually left just one letter off a birthday cake, they would be fired.

Life becomes seriously dangerous when standards are lowered. Using a hammer, crossing a street, slicing a tomato with a knife, managing money are only done successfully by those who have mastered the skill 100 percent. Anything less, and I mean anything less, should not be justified or tolerated. Driving a car with 70 percent competence leaves room for 30 percent disaster.

When masses of children are falsely labeled, often drugged, then given low expectations in school, we cannot expect them to magically become intelligent, contributing adults.

I understand that some children *do* have disabilities. Some children will be dependent on the care of others for their entire lives. Autism, brain damage, etc. do exist. However, we should expect that whatever that child is capable of learning, whatever he or she is capable of doing, whatever he or she is capable of managing, it is done with the goal of mastering it. I don't care if their only skill is putting bay leaves in a spice jar, the skill should be performed with 100 percent accuracy. To do anything less, to expect anything less, robs that child (special needs or not) of their personal sense of pride, accomplishment, and contribution to society.

Thankfully, there are many organizations that employ adults with special needs. In every organization that I have had the honor of working with, the individuals with special needs are treated with kindness and compassion, but they are expected to do their job correctly. Whether it is bagging groceries, moving boxes or greeting people.

The only standard is 100 percent. Anything less is unacceptable.

By the way, I wonder what Helen's Keller's "Measurable Goals" would look like if she had an IEP.

Chapter 7

A Behavioral Specialist's Guide to Bullies

When I hear of a seven or eight-year-old taking their own life because they were relentlessly bullied at school, I always wonder: where were the parents? Where were the teachers? Someone had to know something was going on.

Warning: I consider this chapter to be the most disturbing of this book as I provide exact quotes from a "behavioral specialist" in regard to the topic of bullying. In my opinion, this is a true example of a wolf in sheep's clothing, and I would not let this man walk my dogs, let alone counsel my child.

Bully (noun) a person who habitually seeks to harm or intimidate those whom they perceive as weak or vulnerable. *Every day the playground bully demanded our lunch money.*

Bully (verb) seek to harm, intimidate, or to make (a weaker person) do things against their will by the use of force and/or threats. *She was bullied into taking and sharing improper photos.*

Vulnerable (adjective) easy to attack physically or upset emotionally. *The vulnerable old lady was easy to take advantage of.*

The statistics on bully-related suicide are alarming:
- Suicide is the third leading cause of death among young people, resulting in about 4,400 deaths per year, according to the CDC. For every suicide among young people, there are at least 100 suicide attempts. Over 14 percent of high school students have considered suicide, and almost 7 percent have attempted it.
- According to statistics reported by ABC News, nearly 30 percent

of students are either bullies or victims of bullying, and 160,000 kids stay home from school every day because of fear of bullying.

- Bully victims are between 2 to 9 times more likely to consider suicide than non-victims, according to studies by Yale University.
- Bully-related suicide can be connected to any type of bullying, including physical bullying, emotional bullying, cyberbullying, and sexting, or circulating suggestive or nude photos or messages about a person.

Source: bullyingstatistics.org

Bullies to Buddies, by Izzy Kalman, a behavioral specialist and veteran school psychologist, is a handbook that teaches the "breakthrough

methods" developed by the author to turn one's bullies into friends. The author promises that if one simply follows his advice, one will be able to turn their bullies into buddies.

The book contains a section "What the Experts Say...." with glowing recommendations of the author's techniques. Note: Most of the testimonials are from fellow psychologists, teachers, and school administrators. I did not find one testimonial from a child who "turned a bully into a buddy." Such success stories may exist, but they are not contained in the book.

One testimonial begins: "*I am a licensed clinical social worker and had no idea of a remedy for my child (and neither did his school therapist) until I thankfully came across your program.*" The person describes that his eight-year-old son was bullied in school and it devastated the boy making his life, quote: "a living hell."

The man writes that the ideas his son learned from *Bullies to Buddies* have changed his attitude completely, and "*Now he thinks it ok and enjoys it when his dad (me) teases him.*"

There's a knee-slapping win if I ever heard one! An eight-year-old already being tormented at school has learned to tolerate being teased or verbally abused by his father and he *enjoys* it.

The author has made a living touring the country, implementing his discoveries in schools, and disseminating them to parents, educators and mental health professionals.

I was gifted a copy of the book *Bullies to Buddies* by a parent who thought the methods could be implemented in my school.

The following are direct quotes, including page numbers from this book:

Page 2

We are
animals?

"Do you wonder how kids can be so cruel to you? Does it seem as if they're acting like animals?

"Well, you are right. They are acting like animals. Because they are animals. And so are you. We all are."

Page 5

"Follow these simple instructions and you will begin defeating your bullies right away. Within a week, hardly anyone will bother you, and if they try, they'll feel like losers and quickly stop. Since you won't be getting anyone in trouble, you won't have to worry about that they'll want revenge. When you turn bullies into buddies, the fear of going to school will be over for good. You will be able to go almost anywhere without being afraid.

"Other good things will start happening when you stop being a victim. Life will be brighter, and you will feel calmer, happier and more confident than you have in a long time. Your sense of humor will improve and being around other people will be more fun. Your brothers and sisters will stop fighting with you and will like you better. And your parents will like you better."

Strong claims. Besides appearing to have tackled the "world peace" problem, the author promises that within a week of using his methods, bullying will come to a stop and one will not have to live in fear ever again.

Page 7

"The real reason they bully you is because you get mad and try to stop them. Without realizing it, you are actually making them bully you."

So, anyone who "takes a stand" against a bully is, per the author, making the bully attack. What message does this send? On this same logic, I guess if someone breaks into my home it is my fault for having a home.

Page 8

"You see, they are not calling you 'fatso' because you are fat, or 'four-eyes' because you wear glasses. They really don't care about how you look. All they really care about is having fun. We all like to have fun, and one great way to have fun is to drive someone else crazy."

Page 11

"It's human nature to enjoy driving people crazy."

The Physical Bullying Experiment

"Step 1: Ask a friend or family member to stand next to you. Then say, 'Give me a push.' After they push you, do absolutely nothing but go back and stand next to them. They will probably stand there a bit confused. They may give you another little push, but probably do nothing after that."

And for the conculsion of this experiment: *"This experiment shows that if you do nothing when people provoke you, most of them feel foolish and stop. You win by ending the assault, even though you did absolutely nothing."*

I do not recommend anyone actually try this. Telling a child that they can end an assault by "doing nothing" is a lie.

Page 14

"You probably don't realize it, but there are slaves working for you round-the-clock without even being told to. These slaves are your parents, and possibly your grandparents or other adult relatives."

Parents are children's slaves? Wrong again, Izzy.

Page 15

"There are two ways to get power. They are known as 'the carrot' or 'the stick.'

"The better you get at giving carrots, the less you will need sticks. You will find people like you better, are nicer to you, and do more for you. (And they won't even guess that you are controlling them!)"

Page 28

"We all want power. We all want respect. And we all want to be popular. The difference between bullies and their victims is that bullies are better at getting what they want."

"Bullies are better at getting what they want...." Seriously? But remember folks, this is from a behavioral specialist! He knows what he is talking about.

"We may not want to admit it, but bullies tend to have a trait we admire: courage. What they do may not be smart, but they have the guts to challenge other people."

Page 29

"Your goal is to turn your bullies into buddies. To start that process, all you need to do is begin thinking of them as good. The sooner you do, the quicker you'll start to win."

Page 30

"Remember, the best way to have power today is by offering carrots. If you understand what bullies want and make them happy, they will stop making you miserable. They can even become your friends."

According to this "gem," if a 12-year-old girl gets asked to lift up her dress, she should just do it. She may even end up with a new friend.

Page 36

"If someone calls you stupid, tell yourself they are saying it not because they want to hurt your feelings, but they want to help you be smarter. So how could you be mad at them? Or if they call you a fatso, it is because they are trying to encourage you to go on a diet. So be appreciative."

This illustration appears with the text.

Page 37

"Or if someone tells you to jump off a tall building, you shouldn't do it just because you are considering them friends who love you. But you should tell yourself they must have a very good reason for saying it. Maybe it's their way of hinting that you are acting like a jerk and would do everyone a favor by stopping."

Page 38

"But you want to be a winner, so you must decide to stop being afraid of bullies. Even if they are bigger and stronger than you, don't worry. You aren't in real danger."

How can any adult say this? Maybe Izzy needs to visit a few hospitals and talk to children who "weren't in real danger" yet nearly lost their lives at the hands of a bully.

Page 39

"It's not enough just to stop being scared of people who threaten you. It is also essential not to get mad at them, either, or you'll end up enemies. So be perfectly calm. Don't give them any dirty looks. Smile instead. Tell yourself that people have every right in the world to try to scare you, and you are not going to take this right away from them. Since they're not doing anything wrong, you have no reason to be mad at them. With this attitude, you will discover that people like you and respect you, and that you have no enemies, no matter how small or weak you may be. In fact, if you have no fear and anger, they may even admire you and want to act as your protectors, especially if you are small and weak!

"***Warning***: *There is, of course a chance that someone is so angry with you that he will actually try to harm you physically. How can you judge if you are in real danger or not? Very simply: by asking yourself if the person threatening you has ever injured you or anyone else before.*"

What. The. Hell! Here we find that the right of someone to bully is more important than the right not to be bullied. Then, if things do escalate and you feel you may be physically harmed, just ask yourself if the bully has ever injured someone before.

There is always a first time for everything. A first threat. A first punch. A first beating. How many school shootings have occurred where it was the first and final violent act of the shooter?

Page 42

"*Everyone thinks that in a fight, the first person to hit is the one who started the fight. The truth is that the second person to hit really started the fight! Does this sound nutty? But it's not. It takes two people to make a fight. When someone hits you, there is no fight yet.*

"*It's only when you attack back that a fight erupts! So yes, even though you are the second person to hit, you actually are the one who started the fight.*"

Page 43

"*If you don't want to be the loser and you don't want to have enemies, you must decide not to defend yourself when someone attacks you.*"

Actually, if you don't want to be a loser, don't follow his advice.

Page 44

"*Telling on bullies, except under rare circumstances, is about the worst thing you can do. The best way to make people despise you without actually committing a crime against them is by trying to get them in trouble with the authorities.*"

Page 46

"*When you tell on kids who bother you, you are letting everyone know that you can't handle your bullies by yourself. You are declaring that you are weaker than they are, that they are defeating you, and that you need a grown-up's help to win."*

Where. To. Begin.

This is an evil, evil philosophy developed by an evil, evil man. (And I only used quotes from the first 46 pages; there are 66 more!) Every single page contains grossly misleading advice. Now I understand why children as young as seven take their own lives as a result of bullying. They had no voice. No solution. No one listened. The bully was never disciplined—the victim was!

Bullies to Buddies begins with the statement "we are all animals." This. Is. A. Lie.

Humans are not mere animals. We are a composite of spirit, mind, and body. We believe in a higher power, we worship, we seek to improve ourselves. Animals are different. Telling someone that they are an animal justifies treating one like an animal.

The reference to "parents being slaves" because they "work round-the-clock without being told to" is both insulting and takes parenting from a creative choice to a chore to be suffered.

I went into adulthood wanting eight children. I adore my four children, but not having more remains my biggest life regret. I personally enjoyed all aspects of my children: making them, being pregnant, midnight feedings, watching them grow.

I never once felt like a "slave." I felt financial stress, but the kids were not the source of the stress. Despite landlords raising rent, cars breaking down, hurricanes causing damage that insurance companies refused to cover, broken agreements, divorce, and all the other random annoyances that life brings I never once considered myself a "slave."

Telling a child that bullies have a trait we all admire (courage) is yet another lie. There is nothing "courageous" or "admirable" about verbally or physically harming another.

The author repeats that if one just gives in or does what the bully wants, one will be fine. Don't be disrespectful—hand over your lunch money with a smile. Don't worry about getting injured, you aren't in real danger. If the bully never physically hurt you before, then he or she most likely won't do it now. It will be fine. You'll make friends!

I find the entire philosophy of *Bullies to Buddies* to be a dangerous indoctrination on how to create a "perfect victim" by teaching children to shut up, smile, take it, and not tell.

And anyone who advises a child "not to tell" has something to hide and is a danger to that child. Period.

Going back to page 37, if a person tells another to "jump off a tall building," (essentially, kill themselves), per the author the person making that request must have a valid reason for doing so. The author does not question the bully for suggesting suicide. No, the author wants the victim to understand that the bully must have a really good reason to talk this way. The victim needs to figure out how and why someone else considers them such "a jerk" that the world would be better off without them in it.

We live in a time where people operate on the false idea that it is okay to tear people down, point out all their flaws, expose shortcomings. Unfortunately, social media has taken this practice to a whole other level, with kids humiliating other kids for likes, followers and shares.

Many online bullies suggest that the targeted individual "kill themselves" as they are such "losers" and "jerks."

Sadly, too many children take the advice, leaving behind broken families, who may never understand what led to this irreversible tragic act, forever blaming themselves for what they could have/should have done to prevent what was happening.

My younger brother committed suicide in his late 30s, so I can speak to this topic from personal experience. My brother was far from a saint. I have no idea how involved he was with drugs and alcohol, but I suspect he was minimally a casual user.

That said, I firmly believe my brother had someone in his inner circle who just tormented him daily. Keeping a record of all he did wrong and throwing it in his face often. Pointing out all his faults in some twisted effort to "improve" him. Telling him, in so many words, to do everyone a favor and "jump off a tall building." Told him how much better life would be if he weren't in it.

My brother tried to appease his "bully," offer "carrots." He tried to think of the bully as the "good guy—a friend—just looking out for my brother's best interest."

My brother tried to improve, tried to measure up. He took a hard look at his value as a father, husband, son and brother. He looked at his value as a man. The problem was he looked at all of these things through the eyes of his bully.

My brother decided that the world was better off without him so hung himself, leaving behind three beautiful children under the age of seven. Children who have no idea that a year prior to his suicide I opened my home to him in Miami for as long as he needed. Children who have no idea that after his death I offered to raise them, knowing there was a zero percent chance I'd be given custody.

Three weeks after my brother's suicide my father succumbed to cancer. We all knew my dad was on borrowed time. He knew he was at the end of life. My brother should have been there for my dad (and my mom). It was no secret that David was the favorite. David was everything to my father. A champion of every sport he ever played, a fishing buddy, a boy who grew to become a handsome, towering, six-foot-five man (looking like Ben Affleck), a person to watch sports with.

Cancer took my father's life; however, it was the loss of David that just broke him.

In memory of David

Chapter 8

Lab Rats and Behavioral Strategies

As mentioned earlier, once my homeschool activity became a private school I began to get contacted by various agencies, offering various services for children. I was approached by individuals offering after school chess clubs, sewing classes, or an afternoon class on robotics using LEGO bricks.

Then came the child advocates, the experts, the therapists, the child psychologists. The wolves in sheep's clothing. All essentially drug pushers in need of more young minds and young bodies to chemically alter and shut down.

Florida International University (FIU) and Funded Drug Studies

Per their current website, FIU's Center for Children and Families is involved in 58 active research projects totaling $94.5 million in federal funding. They provide, per them, "the highest quality care for children and adolescents affected by mental illness." The head psychiatrist is Dr. William E. Pelham, Jr.

I have crossed paths with FIU's Center for Children and Families on several occasions. I have enrolled at my school a handful of students who previously attended an FIU behavioral modification program, or who have been part of a research study involving medication.

Even though I have only ever enrolled a handful of children who were part of an FIU research study or camp, I am not at all impressed with FIU's tactics and results.

Examining Tolerance to CNS Stimulant Medication in ADHD—An FIU Research Study under Dr. Pelham.

Reese was in the seventh grade when she enrolled at H.E.L.P. Miami. (The Hollywood Education & Literacy Project is the name of the private school I founded.) She enrolled one month before Christmas break. Reese was taking medication as part of the FIU's "Examining Tolerance to CNS Stimulant Medication in ADHD" research project.

Our first action was to have her take a complete battery of TerraNova academic tests to see where she placed. She tested at a third grade level (four grades behind in reading, language and math).

Before the end of Reese's first week, I was contacted by a woman from FIU, asking for my cooperation in monitoring Reese for side-effects to current medication. I refused to participate as I am an educator, not a qualified medical doctor.

The woman, Lisa, insisted that Reese had excelled in their program but did not have a response when I questioned the psychiatric definition of the "progress" considering that Reese was four grade levels behind and on her third medication.

Lisa said that she respected my position not to monitor pharmaceutical side-effects but mailed me a packet of forms in case I changed my mind.

The packet was eight pages with the first page entitled, "**Teacher Reimbursement Form.**" FIU was going to give me (or Reese's teacher) financial compensation for time spent monitoring and reporting side-effects to medication.

Here is a copy of the letter I sent to Dr. Pelham about this student:

William E. Pelham, Jr., Ph.D.
Director, Center for Children and Families FIU

CC: Parents of Reese Doe

10 December 2014

Dear Dr. Pelham,

I wanted to take a moment to respond to the fax asking for H.E.L.P. Miami's cooperation in the "Examining Tolerance to CNS Stimulant Medication in ADHD" study that seventh grade student Reese Doe is a participant in.

I want to make it very clear that H.E.L.P. Miami, its teachers or administrative staff, will take no part in the above named study. We will not fill out behavior monitoring checklists or do monthly "five-minute ratings" in exchange for $100 as we feel that medicating children for academic problems is not scientifically proven to solve academics and may be potentially dangerous to the child consumer.

Personally, I challenge the statement: "The medication was shown to be helpful for Reese based on measures of behavior and classroom performance during the Summer Treatment Program." Though Reese only recently enrolled I have not noticed any issue with her behavior. However, she was given a complete battery of academic tests upon her November 5, 2014 enrollment. (Test scores are attached.) Scores show Reese to be at 3.1 overall grade level.

Her teacher confirms that she is performing below grade level in the core subjects of reading, language arts and math. I respectfully ask how testing four grades below level is an indication of classroom improvement?

Further, I question the stated purpose of the said study: "To determine whether children develop 'tolerance' to stimulant medications prescribed for ADHD such that the medication stops working as well over time as it does initially."

Essentially, Reese is being used as a "lab rat" to test how she "tolerates" various psychotropic medications. I do not see how altering Reese's central nervous system using CNS medications will result in her mastering academics and growing into an independent, intelligent, thriving woman.

As you can tell, I am quite passionate about this topic. In 25 years of being an educator, I have lost two of my students to cardiac arrest and suicide which were later determined to be side-effects of the medication they were taking for ADHD. Parents of other students say their children were left with permanent liver damage, tremors, digestive problems, and so on, related to ADHD medication.

To date, I have helped over 700 children (who were labeled "learning disabled") overcome their academic difficulties and win at study. This is consistently done with tutoring, small classes, individualized attention from teachers, ensuring that the student masters skills before moving on and by insisting the student can correctly define terms they encounter in each subject. Structuring the school with small classes allows every student to get the attention needed and also allows our teachers to have a positive impact on their students. Documented success stories, improved test scores, and the fact that over 80 percent of my high school graduates (many who were diagnosed with ADHD) are in college shows that our system is workable.

I am confident that H.E.L.P. Miami can help Reese get on track as a student, but only by using the method we have consistently found successful.

Yours,

Barbara Brown Rivera, Founder and Director HELP Miami (helpmiami.org)

I never received a response to this letter.

Despite the letter refusing my participation in monitoring medication and the previous phone call, FIU still pursued me. I will never forget the phone call, as it was the last day of school before Christmas break. The school was buzzing with "Santa Claus and visions of sugarplums." My little ones were playing Rudolf Bingo and my high school students were wearing elf ears and singing "Hotel California" on a Karaoke machine. I was in the middle of some candy cane craft when I was informed, "Lisa from FIU is on the phone. She wants to discuss a research study she needs your help with."

Shaking my head and rolling my eyes, I went to my office with my adult son, Damon, right behind me. My side of the conversation went like this:

"Thank you. And Merry Christmas to you, Lisa. I am in the middle of a school Christmas party so do not have much time... No, I haven't changed my mind."

(Damon passes me a note—*"Tell Lisa to go to hell!"*)

"No Lisa. I am not on board with medication. I have told you my reasons. No, I get it, but that is not what I do..."

(Damon rewrites the same note, using all capital letters—*"TELL LISA TO GO TO HELL!"*

"Lisa, it is not about the money. I am just not..."

(Damon underlines the word HELL three times and I try to grab his pen.)

"Lisa. I am not participating. Period. You can talk to Reeses' parents— they know my stance. They can medicate their daughter as they see fit... I am just not going help to monitor the..."

(Damon writes another note in even larger letters: SEND LISA TO HELL! DO IT FOR CHRISTMAS!)

"I completely understand, but there is nothing you can say that will get me to change my mind..."

(Damon, who was pacing at this point, writes: MOM! In 8-inch letters, underlining each letter three times, making an angry face complete with devil-horns in the letter "O".)

"Lisa, I have to go. Yes, have a happy New Year, too. No, I don't need more time to think about this over the holiday. Lisa, I have made it very clear."

Thankfully, Lisa hung up as I was about to lose it. During the ten-minute conversation, I had little ones coming to my office to show off paper snowmen they made and my high school boys were now singing "Staying Alive" by the Bee Gees with full gusto. If Lisa or Dr. Pelham had walked into my school, we probably all would have been committed.

But how thick can one be? I only repeated myself about 35 times. I was even polite about it.

Makes me want to start a "No Means No Research Study for College Professionals who try to Hard-Sell others to Drug Children". I am going to ask for more than $94.5 million in federal funds. I'll give Damon a few million to invest in a line of T-shirts that read: Go to hell, Lisa!

By the way, Lisa never called back. Probably because the parents withdrew their daughter from the FIU research study. It took us a year or so to get her up to grade level. Not the smoothest journey, but she did it.

Ineffective Behavioral Strategies

My high school students are taught to spot and question sweeping generalities, as these generalities are often based on opinion, not actual fact. A statement such as, "Smoking is bad for one's health" may be obvious; however, one should ask, "How is it bad?" "What are the facts about smoking?" "What exactly does smoking do to the body?" Otherwise, it is a general statement—even if believable, it still needs to be backed up with actual facts. Actual evidence.

A former high school graduate had a part-time job as camp counselor at a Parks and Recreation after-school program. Part of on-going staff training included a slideshow presentation by FIU's Center for Children and Families.

This student called me immediately after the presentation in disbelief of what she just witnessed. Thankfully, each attendee received a printed copy of the presentation to refer to. My student asked for an extra copy of the slideshow to pass on to me.

The FIU presentation was 32 slides in length, including the title and end slide, prompting the audience to ask questions. Many of the slides contained one image or questions for the audience to think about. I am going to share four slides, including the title here:

Effective Behavior Management
Erika K. Coles, Ph.D
Center for Children and Families
Florida International University

Slide 9

Causes of ADHD?
- Chronic, neurobiological disorder
- Causes are unknown
- Has genetic/hereditary components
- Prenatal environment can increase risk
- Mother's nutrition and stress level
- Exposure to lead and pesticides

Things that DO NOT Cause ADHD
- Poor parenting
- Single parenting
- Watching TV
- Vaccines
- Food additives
- Too much sugar

I do not know the context of the "Causes of ADHD?" but I find the section listed under "Things that DO NOT Cause ADHD" to be sweeping generalities. I also find them, based on my personal experience, to be false.

Poor parenting does affect the behavior of a child. Sitting for hours in front of a TV (versus playing outdoors, building things, participating in sports, reading, art, dance, and so on), does affect a child. Quality of food does affect a child. Sugar does affect a child. And I personally know of one child who the parent claims was damaged by a vaccine. (The boy was normal one day, then completely disconnected after getting a shot.)

No studies are listed to support the claims. FIU is issuing a statement and we are supposed to accept it as fact.

Slide 10

Effective Interventions for Behavior Problems

- **Behavior Modification**
  - Home (Parenting strategies)
  - School (Classroom behavior management)
  - Intensive summer camps
- **Medication**
  - Stimulants (Ritalin, Concerta, Adderall)
  - Straterra
- **Combined Behavior Modification and Medication**

Are we surprised that medication is mentioned as effective?

Slide 11

Interventions that are Not Effective for ADHD and behavior problems

- One-on-one supportive counseling
- Play therapy
- Elimination diets
- Biofeedback
- Allergy treatments
- Chiropractics
- Sensory integration
- Karate

Again, where are the studies? How did FIU determine allergy treatments were ineffective? How many kids with allergies and ADHD were researched? Who were the chiropractors involved in the study? What did they say about ADHD?

These are all blatant generalities with no hard evidence as support. Just because someone with a degree and a white coat makes a statement does not mean that statement is true.

Slide 31 goes into the step-by-step way to manage "mildly annoying behavior." This is how the professionals, the child experts, with degrees and certification, handle poor behavior.

Ignore Mildly Annoying Behavior
- No eye contact (Don't look)
- No verbal contact (Don't talk)
- Remove other attention (peers)
- Praise peers who are ignoring the behavior
- Ignore to the end
- Then praise alternative behavior
  - I like how you're sitting quietly now. How can I help?

Do not engage—avoid the "trap"

When Jimmy is displaying mildly annoying behavior the expert advice is to not look at him and then don't talk to him. Then we are to continue not looking and not talking until, magically, Jimmy decides to stop acting like a little punk at which time we then praise him.

On what planet does this work?

I am expected to believe that if my boys are clowning around in the kitchen, instead of washing the dishes they are flicking each other with dish towels, I should just ignore them, not say anything and somehow my boys will decide on their own to stop acting like fools and get the dishes done. I don't think so.

As a parent and as a principal, I can tell you that the only way to correct a misbehaving child is to look them in the eyes and talk directly to them. One does not need to be mean about it, but one should be firm.

Enough Is Enough!

Here is a copy of my letter to FIU about their Effective Behavior Management presentation:

Center for Children and Families
Florida International University
11200 SW 8th Street
AHC 1 Room 140
Miami, Florida 33199

13 April 2015

Dear Ms. Erika Coles,

I would like to request disclosure on a research study in which you are involved named Effective Behavior Management. As part of a Power Point presentation given by you, it is asserted that the following are not effective for ADHD and behavior problems:

• One-on-one supportive therapy
• Allergy treatments
• Play therapy
• Chiropractics
• Elimination diets
• Sensory integration
• Biofeedback
• Karate

I would like the scientific evidence that shows conclusively that the above are in fact "ineffective." Who did the research? How many children were involved in the research? Which chiropractors were part of the study? Over what period of time was the research done? How many allergy tests were performed, and to what result? And so on for each point listed.

Further, I would like scientific proof that medication is effective in treating behavior problems. What is the biological compound that has been found that causes behavior problems? If the child is found to have a chemical imbalance, what is the name of the chemical, where is it located in the body and at what level or percentage was the child chemically imbalanced? What specific medical test is performed to test for chemical imbalance? How many children prescribed medications were cured? How many children no longer need medication? What other behavior therapies were used?

One of the final panels on the Effective Behavior Management Power Point is titled: Ignore Mildly Annoying Behavior. The first two points listed are:

• No eye contact (Don't look)
• No verbal contact (Don't talk)

This panel goes on to state that you "ignore (mildly annoying behavior) to the end."

As an educator and a parent, I completely disagree with the "the no eye contact/no verbal contact" method of addressing children who are misbehaving (mildly or not so mildly). Telling any adult that the treatment of children is based on "not communicating" to them is not only wrong, it is unintelligent.

Again, I would like the scientific proof that this "no eye contact/no verbal contact" is effective. What study was done to prove this? How many children were "ignored to the end" and overcame their "mildly annoying" behavior?

If you cannot provide scientific evidence, supported by real statistics, then I kindly ask that you cease using this Power Point as it clearly is pro-pharmaceutical and, I believe, not only false but potentially harmful in content.

I look forward to hearing from you.

Yours,
Barbara Rivera, Founder & Director
HELP Miami (helpmiami.org)

I never heard from Dr. Coles or any of the psychiatrists or psychologists posted at FIU. (And I have sent a few letters over the years.)

However, a new presentation has been created. The presentation in its entirety can be found and downloaded from FIU's Center for

Children and Families website. Here are a few slides:

Slide 1

Current Views of the Best Treatments
for ADHD: A Decade-Plus of Research
on Comparing, Combining & Sequencing
Interventions for Childhood ADHD
William E. Pelham, Jr. PhD ABPP
Center for Children and Families

Florida International University
CCF Webinar (Center for Children and
Families)
October 29, 2020

Slide 22

Evidence-Based Short-Term Treatments for
ADHD
    1. Behavior Modification -hundreds of
    studies
    2. CNS Stimulant Medication -hundreds of
    studies
    3. The combination on (1) and (2) > 30+
    Studies
Moderate to large effect sizes across
treatments

"*Hundreds of studies*" is just another generality and is a joke of a statement. This would be like someone saying, "Red cars are best—hundreds of studies." Of course they find medication to be a valid treatment for ADHD—they are funded to use ADHD medication! How stupid does FIU think we are?

Here is a statement for their next presentation: FIU's Center for Children and Families is full of Meatheads— hundreds of studies.

What I want to know is with $94 million in funding how many children were actually *cured – or even helped?*

The following three slides taken directly from FIU's website are very telling:

Slide 27

Psychoactive Medication Business is Booming in America
"Insurance plans now spend more money on psychotropics than antibiotics or asthma meds, with ADHD being the leading cost."

Slide 35

Despite the Evidence, Medication is Universally Used as First-Line Treatment for ADHD in the U.S.

A Risk Benefit Analysis shows clearly that Behavior Therapy (BT) has Lower Risks (Side Effects) and Equivalent Efficacy so BT should Routinely be the First Line Treatment for ADHD

Translation: The United States prescribes medication first, even though studies find Behavior Therapy to have lower risks and to be just as effective as medication.

Slide 90

Conclusions
- No beneficial effect of long-acting stimulant medication (Concerta) on homework completion or accuracy
- Significant beneficial effect (e.g., "C" performance to "B" performance) of group BPT focused on parent's structuring and overseeing child's homework
- No incremental value of adding medication to the homework-focused BPT

BPT (Behavioral Parent Training)

Draw your own conclusions, but it looks to me like Dr. Pelham's own research is conclusive that ADHD medications are not proven to work! He also "concludes" that when a parent helps their child with homework (structuring and overseeing), the child does better.

My grandmother with only a sixth grade education could have told you that kids do better in school when parents help them with homework. (And she would not have required a $94 million grant to do so.)

Interviewing Psychiatrists by a Hotel Pool

In 2006 or 2007, the Psychiatric Association had their annual Youth Psychiatric Convention at the Omni Hotel on Miami Beach. I went with a friend, as I had a few questions.

I did not get pushy or throw a fit or get aggressive. I truly wanted to know a few things. My friend and I went to the Omni and hung out by the pool, waiting for the upcoming session break. Soon the patio was full of about 30 psychiatrists in beach attire, some still had their IDs.

Casually, I introduced myself saying my friend and I were in town for a wedding. Then, as if planned, the psychiatrist would introduce himself or herself and say they were attending the psychiatric youth convention.

I swear to you, I was nothing but nice. Here is one conversation:

Me: "*May I tell you something that I have heard on TV?*"

Male Psychiatrist: "*Sure.*"

Me: "*I've heard that there actually isn't a scientific test to determine if a child has ADHD. Is this true?*"

Male Psychiatrist: "*There is no test at this time. We make good guesses based on a number of factors and observations. The science is evolving and we hope to have this nailed down soon.*"

Me: "*What about a test for chemical imbalance? How can you tell if there is too much or too little of a chemical?*"

Male Psychiatrist: "*Again, there is no test.*"

Me: "*What is the name of the chemical that could be imbalanced?*"

Male Psychiatrist: "*The exact chemical has not been isolated.*"

Me: "*So how can you tell what treatment to use?*"

Male Psychiatrist: "*We make an educated guess. This is why people usually end up taking multiple medications as we need to find what works for the patient.*"

Me: "*But if I had high blood pressure and my friend had low blood pressure, we would not be prescribed the same drug, right?*"

Male Psychiatrist: "*Correct. Blood pressure can be exactly monitored.*"

Me: "*Got it. How many people do you think you've cured in your career?*"

Male Psychiatrist: "*Well that is a good question. We have found that in the field of ADHD and mental health, symptoms can be managed but generally people cannot be cured.*"

· § ·

I talked to another psychiatrist whose job was developing drugs for pharmaceutical companies.

Me: "*If you don't have children to test the drugs on, who do you use?*"

Male Psychiatrist: "*Lesser animals. Rats are the go-to choice as they have similarities to humans.*"

Me: "*Well, if you ever find a rat that can raise children and do housework, please send him my way.*"

I spoke to several psychiatrists that day. Kept it very casual. Each confirmed that there was no test for ADHD or behavioral disorders. Each confirmed that there was no actual evidence to support the "chemical imbalance" theory.

I did not challenge them further. I wanted to have short, relaxed, casual conversations and I got exactly that.

And my friend got it all on tape.

Crossing Paths with Florida International University Again

On August 22, 2019, I was a guest speaker on The Addiction Podcast—Point of No Return. The podcast features former addicts, parents who lost a child to drugs, politicians, police officers and drug rehab professionals. The host chose to interview me on the subject of ADHD medications as many of her previous guests stated that they felt their "addiction" problems began when they were placed on psychotropics for learning disabilities. During the show I spoke about the financial kick-backs, gift cards and incentives offered by FIU to monitor side-effects of medication or to participate in a research study.

A few months after the podcast aired, I was contacted by the producer of The Addiction Podcast, stating that a journalist contacted the show about the information I shared on my episode.

The journalist decided to do an independent investigation into FIU by contacting Dr. William Pelham via email. The communication from the journalist was non-confrontational and friendly. The doctor was questioned about offering financial kick-backs to teachers and families. He adamantly denied my claim, stating I was misinformed and basically spreading "lies" about his work.

The journalist continued the email thread by asking the doctor for specifics: "What exactly was Barbara Rivera saying that was false?"

Dr. Pelham refused to answer further questions stating that all further communication should be directed to the legal department of FIU.

The journalist then reached out to the Addiction Podcast for my contact information.

I was able to provide her copies of actual documents that more than support the statements made by me.

This is a quote directly from a promotional postcard sent to families and schools from FIU:

"Some families receive free counseling sessions designed to help teens and parents make informed decisions about ADHD treatment. Participating families may earn up to $200 in gift cards over 2 years for completing

questionnaires and other study-related tasks."

This same promise of gift cards appears plain as day on FIU billboards around the city.

I shared a copy of an FIU CCF (Center for Children and Families) letter, dated December 1, 2014, signed by Dr. Pelham. This was addressed to one of my teachers, requesting their participation in a drug study on one of our students. The letter goes over the protocols of said study which includes this paragraph:

"We will contact you every 4 weeks to obtain your monthly behavior ratings. At the end of the school year, we will ask you to complete a brief set of behavior rating scales. You will receive a $100 gift card for completing these ratings during the year."

I shared yet another FIU CCF letter, dated August 10, 2009, signed by Wendy K. Silverman, Director and Professor of Psychology. (This was a letter sent to all school counselors in the area.) The letter states:

"We financially compensate all families for their participation in our comprehensive assessments. Because CAPP (Child Anxiety and Phobia Program) is a clinical-research facility, the fee for treatment is nominal. Families who cannot afford the fees of private practitioners or who lack insurance are especially appropriate."

I have no idea if the journalist went forward with her story or not, but she was given enough proof that FIU CCF does offer financial kick-backs.

As for FIU, I'd be interested in how many children overcame their learning problems or behavior disorders to become stable, well-adjusted, contributing members of society.

If I can successfully raise and homeschool four children on my own, on a single mother's income, with no degree or formal education, then I feel I have the right to expect the same or more from a university program run by behavioral experts and funded with over $94 million.

Foster Parent Certification

As mentioned earlier, I always wanted a big family. Seven or eight children would have been ideal for me. Several factors, which I touch upon later, prevented me adding to the family. However, around 2011 with my own children all grown and out of the house, I decided to get certified as a foster parent. My intention was not to foster but to adopt. I made this known on the application, stating that I was seeking to adopt siblings, age and race were not an issue, though I preferred not to take on an infant. I wanted the kids to be older.

I would just do what worked for my children: a schedule, nice clothes, plenty of art supplies, books, and age-appropriate chores. We'd prepare dinner together and sit down as a family discussing the day, who and how we helped and anything else of interest. We'd go for walks, play board games and maybe buy a hamster. I planned that the kids would go to my school.

I did the weekly classes, filled out all the documents, made a photo album of myself and my children, my children were given questionnaires to see how they'd respond to getting siblings (they were all on board), and finally, I ended up certified.

To make a long story short, there were plenty of siblings in the age range I wanted. Two, three and even four brothers and sisters looking for a home. I never actually met any of the children as it turns out that all of them were on multiple medications. When I voiced that I wanted to get the children off the drugs, even giving the name of a qualified pediatrician who would help me, I was told that the children were "court-ordered" to be on drugs and if I did anything to violate the court order, I could go to jail.

And that was enough for me to drop the issue. My takeaway: the "system" would rather see children on drugs than potentially thriving in a stable household.

More on the "Don't Do Anything" Approach

Project RISE (funded by the Children's Trust) is another South Florida program that is designed to help youth organizations rise to meet the health, safety, academic and social-emotional needs of the children they serve.

Project RISE reached out to me years ago, offering their reading program. I declined. I had successes in teaching reading so why fix something that isn't broken?

They sent me a promotional packet in case I changed my mind at a future date. The packet contained a copy of a presentation on helping a student read that I assume was delivered to groups of educators.

The reading presentation was written by someone who could turn a task like "giving a dog water" into an 85-page PowerPoint, using only five syllable words with Venn diagrams in font size 6. It was almost comical in how complex and serious it was. But as I mentioned, I was happy with my reading program, so I filed the Project RISE reading presentation in a folder marked "stupid stuff."

Then I opened the information packet titled:

Tools for Managing Challenging Behaviors in the OOS (Out of School) Setting

Per Project RISE, here are the steps to deal with a child exhibiting "attention seeking behaviors:"

Briefly remove all attention from the misbehaving child

- Turn your head and avoid eye contact
- Refuse to touch, talk, argue, scold, or look at the child while they are engaging in the behavior
- Don't show anger in your manner or gesture
- Pretend to be absorbed in some other activity

In other words, the "expert's advice" is to ignore the child and do absolutely nothing.

I challenge the practice of "ignoring" bad behavior. If a child is acting out (mildly or not so mildly) that child needs eye contact, verbal direction, and consequences that fit the circumstance. Period.

I have encountered three different incidents of girls, aged 13 to 16, who were sending nude photos of themselves to male classmates. These incidents were years apart and completely separate from each other. Thankfully, in all three incidents, the boys wasted no time reporting this to their parents and then to me.

Interestingly enough, each girl happened to be receiving psychological counseling and, in each case, the "professional advice" was to "ignore" the girls' behavior. Let them "work it out for themselves."

My non-professional advice to the parents was to take a hammer to all the devices. Destroy the phone, iPads, etc. The girls can get a job, buy their own electronics, and pay for the service. Until then, do not finance their immoral, dangerous behavior.

My advice, which I still consider valid, was met with harsh backlash from the psychologists and families involved.

"My child will not fit in with her peers if she does not have a phone!" *"How is she supposed to socialize?"*

One mother, following recommendations of the family psychologist, withdrew her daughter from my school due to my attitude.

Bottom line, all of the girls kept their phones and continued sharing naked pictures on platforms hidden from the parents.

Ignoring the bad behavior did not result in good behavior. Ignoring a problem never solves a problem.

I once had a ten-year-old boy who teased a classmate to tears (calling her fat). First offense, the boy was in my office. He was spoken to in a firm but fair manner. No one has the right to make another cry. The boy apologized to me and the girl. The next day, this little thug was at it again. *"Fatty, fatty, fatty,"* said under his breath, but overheard by a teacher. The girl was in tears again and the boy had an accomplished smirk on his face.

Well, that smirk and attitude were not going to be ignored. I called the girl's father, explained the situation, and asked him to come to school. He arrived within an hour.

As mentioned earlier, my office has wall-to-wall windows, allowing me an unobstructed view out and students an unobstructed view in.

The dad walked into my "one-room schoolhouse," and his daughter said, "Hi, Daddy." He walked over and kissed her then took a seat in my office and I called the troublemaker in. The whole school got quiet anticipating what was about to go down.

The boy came in, I shut the door, politely introduced him to the girl's father, then asked him to tell the man what he calls his daughter. The boy froze.

"Go on. Tell Mr. Garcia how you treat his daughter. What exactly do you say that makes her cry?"

Brutal.

It took a few minutes, but the boy eventually came clean.

The father handled this so well. (I knew he would; otherwise, I would not have had him confront the boy.) The dad nicely explained that his daughter is the most important person in the world to him. And that he loves her very much. He said she loves this school and is doing so well. He did not want her to cry or be bullied or made fun of.

The father told the boy that real men do not abuse women or girls. Real men stand up for women and girls.

He got the boy to agree to stop teasing his daughter, be her friend, help her with schoolwork. They even shook hands on it.

The boy kept his promise, not only looking out for the girl, but he looked out for all girls (and boys). My other students also learned not to tease by example as they knew the consequences. For the next few months, my students were extra polite to each other. And extra polite to their teachers.

Ignoring the taunts. Not looking at the boy. Not calling the boy out on his rude behavior could have resulted in more bullying and ruined the self-esteem of a little girl. Looking at him, talking directly to him, holding him accountable for his actions resulted in a change of behavior. It may have saved him a lot of trouble down the road.

The Ultimate Price of Ignoring Bad Behavior

On September 8, 2019, the New York Post published a story about a South Florida student. Here are a few highlights:

> On Nov. 4, after two months of gathering "data" for Cruz's "Functional Behavior Assessment," teachers were sent his "Positive Behavior Intervention Plan." The plan included helpful tips, like:
>
> If Nikolas destroys property at a lower level,
>
> • Calmly let him know he has not followed one of the expectations. Remind him what he is working for.
> • Prompt him to use a cool down pass and walk away to diffuse [sic] the situation.
>
> If Nikolas engages in major disruption/property destruction:
>
> • Let Nikolas know, "You're getting too loud. I need for you to get back into control by using a cool down pass or calming down at your desk. If you get back into control, you can stay in class. If you continue, I'll need for you leave [sic]."
> • Walk away and do not pay attention to his behavior.
> • Do not argue with Nikolas or engage with him.
> • When class is over, Nikolas needs to go to his next class and behavior plan should re-set with able to [sic] earn reward breaks again.

Teachers were required to implement this plan for at least six weeks until Cruz could become eligible for further evaluation.

In late November, Cruz attempted to commit suicide at school by running into oncoming traffic. But that did not accelerate the process. School administrators classified the incident as "minor disruption."

February 14, 2018, Nikolas Cruz shot 34 students and staff, murdering 17 at Parkland High School, located about 40 minutes from where I live. This tragedy could have been prevented.

Nikolas had a history of exhibiting bad behavior which went ignored. Staff were instructed (in writing) by behavioral experts to walk away, not to argue, not to give him attention, not to engage. This Behavioral Strategy failed.

Normal people look directly at their child when they act out. Normal people talk directly to their child when they misbehave. When bad behavior is permitted and encouraged to go unchecked, we end up with chaos. In the case of Nikolas Cruz, it resulted in the loss of innocent lives. People sent their kids to school that day and they did not come home. Adults went to work that day and they did not come home.

Ignoring bad behavior does not work with babies. It does not work with children. It does not work with adults. It does not work with pets.

It has been my experience as a parent, teacher, principal, dog owner and human being that in order to survive at all, one must have eyes in the back of their head and use this ability to maintain order.

Thinking that children will improve when ignored is a complete falsehood. Rudeness, bad behavior, bullying, and crime should not be tolerated. It should be dealt with directly.

I'd much rather incorrectly discipline a child than not use discipline at all. If I blame the wrong child for something, I can and should apologize. But to see or hear something wrong and not take some action is insane.

The effects of this insanity can be seen in everyday life: stores getting looted, teachers no longer permitted to maintain order in their classroom, police getting attacked, and outright murder (just to name a few) are occurring daily.

And who is behind it?

The only people pushing a "don't look/don't talk/ignore" ideology are the psychologists and psychiatrists. This and the drugs they push speak volumes to their true intentions towards our children, our country, and mankind.

Chapter 9

Textbooks, Assignments, Daily Homework

Common Core

It is no secret that Common Core is considered an epic failure. From my experience, when an "education" fails, one is quick to blame politicians, or lack of school funding, or fatherless homes (all of which may be valid). In my opinion, Common Core would still be an epic failure even if there were intact families, fully funded schools with the best teachers and peace on Earth.

I am not going to speak to any political agendas behind Common Core or what or who made billions off of its nationwide implementation. I am going to share actual examples of Common Core materials so you can judge for yourself if this is an effective teaching curriculum.

I became very familiar with Common Core textbooks from students I tutored who needed help with math and reading. These children attended public, private or charter schools and were using textbooks stamped with *"Aligns to Common Core State Standards," "Common Core Edition,"* or something to that effect.

I will not lie, Common Core books looked fantastic. Their covers featured bold colors with sharks, jaguars, or kids on skateboards. Very high quality. Then I opened the book and started to read.

I found the material so complex and convoluted it was a challenge for me to figure out. Definitions were invented seemingly out of thin air, such as defining the number 6 as a "double" because if one "doubles the digit 3, as in 3 + 3" one gets 6. A simple problem like "8 x 4" was turned into a multi-step mental exercise, demanding detailed written explanations and diagrams.

The word "homonym" has been replaced with the word "homogram." (Homonyms are words that are spelled or pronounced the same but have different meanings such as the word "bat," which can be an animal or a stick used in baseball.)

I recall tutoring a fourth grader on a Common Core science packet about the circulatory system written as if the child was already a practicing heart surgeon. Seriously, about 17 medical terms were crammed into two paragraphs making the subject impossible to grasp.

I found the same needlessly complicated approach in writing, reading and grammar.

I once spoke to a certified teacher who was pro-Common Core. This woman stated that Common Core emphasized the use of questioning to promote and develop "critical thinking" skills.

"Critical thinking" is defined as "observing something so one can make a judgment about it."

I think demanding that a child write a paragraph explaining how he or she knows $2 + 3 = 5$ ruins math.

I think the mind develops critical thinking naturally.

A toddler sees car keys and puts them in his/her mouth. Later, the same individual will use the car keys to drive a car. Somewhere along the line, as a natural progression of growth, the individual figured out the purpose of car keys. Trying to give a toddler a lesson on keys would be useless and probably very frustrating for the toddler and the teacher.

My personal four children were taught what could now be called "old-school math." They learned to add, subtract, multiply and divide *expertly*. This skill helped them win board games, sell lemonade, bake cupcakes, and manage their birthday money. Not once did I attempt to develop critical thinking by making things almost impossible to understand. My children were taught a skill, in the simplest form I could find, then given many opportunities to use (think with and apply) said skill in real life.

My argument is that I feel that over-complicated material (complete with psychological questioning) shuts down one's critical thinking ability. It shuts down one's natural wish to learn.

In a matter of a few years, I noticed that the kids who grew up using Common Core books were further and further behind. Sixth graders did not know the times tables, ninth graders did not know how to write a proper sentence or how to identify parts of speech.

Pearson was (and still is) the top publisher for educational textbooks worldwide. They provide materials for pre-schools all the way to college. Pearson's curriculum comes in the form of textbooks, lesson plans and multimedia programs. Pearson publishes under several titles such as Scott Foresman, Prentice Hall, Addison-Wesley, Peachpit, to name a few.

Pearson had the exclusive rights to develop the Common Core curriculum.

In addition to educational materials, Pearson's name appears on the BASC-2 (Behavioral Assessment System for Children, Second Edition). This is a psychological checklist that has 150 characteristics used by the parent or teacher to rate the child. I am sure they publish other mental health or ADHD screening checklists.

In 2013 Pearson acquired the assets of an ADHD testing company called BioBehavioral Diagnostics.

Pearson produces curriculum that is, in my opinion, deliberately confusing. Students using these materials start failing. Pearson has forms used to diagnose said student with various learning or behavioral disorders. They even have the laboratories to develop the meds.

Samples of Second Grade Math

Read these three problems from beginning to end. If you are confused, imagine how an eight-year-old feels.

Problem 1:

Add 26 + 17 by breaking apart numbers to make a ten.

Use a number that adds with 6 in 26 to make a 10.

Since 6 + 4 = 10, use 4.

Think 17 = 4 + 13.

Add 26 + 4 = 30.

Add 30 + 13 = 43.

So, 26 + 17 = 43.

Problem 2:

Tell how to make 10 when adding 8 + 5.
The student is then required to write a paragraph explaining how they arrived at their answer.

Problem 3:

7 x 7 = 7 x (5 + _____)

= (_____ x 5) + (7 x _____)

= _____ – _____

= _____

The student is instructed to write all multiplication problems in this ridiculous Common Core fashion. Students who do not follow this methodology will be marked wrong, even if the student got the correct answer.

Phonics

Look at the following samples of phonics. The first image comes from a phonics workbook from the 1970s. The purpose of the page is obvious. The student is learning to identify letter "p" and recognize objects that begin with the "p" sound. The student reviews earlier letters learned by writing the letter each picture begins with. There are no directions as the author understands that the child cannot read at this stage. This simple exercise done in volume will take a child from knowing the alphabet and letter sounds to reading.

The next image came from an on-line search for Common Core Phonics.

And the final one is a flashcard that goes with the image from the Common Core Phonics.

Old-school phonics that work.

The student is presented words he or she cannot read. When we look at teaching a child the sound the letter "k" makes, the "k" in the word "knee" is silent. Second, do we really need to "kill" a seemingly happy dragon? Try explaining "kidneys" to a five-year-old or getting them to pronounce "kookaburra." This type of work done in volume will produce a frustrated child and teacher. It would have been far more effective to use words familiar to a child such as: kitten, king, or kangaroo.

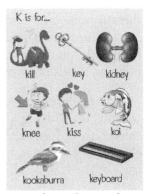

Modern phonics that don't work.

Additional Subjects

I literally have stacks and stacks of Common Core materials assigned to students of all grades that mirror the above. No subject has been spared. From the altered facts, to having some psychological or political message shoved down someone's throat, the material taught in modern schools is no longer about the "A, B, Cs or 1, 2, 3s."

I have seen a language arts assignment intended for a second grader that deals with a wife discovering her husband is cheating. The assignment asked the student to write

This is just unbelievably awful.

answers to questions about the wife's emotions and what she should do.

I have seen vocabulary words to accompany a lesson on "police brutality" for middle schoolers.

Just Google "McGraw Hill's slavery quote" and you'll see for yourself what is being printed in textbooks.

This is not education. This is indoctrination masquerading as "education."

These assignments and many like them do not result in a child being able to come to their own conclusions. The content potentially puts a child in doubt about the security of his or her family (as in the assignment about infidelity) or plants the idea that "police are bad." I believe these are dangerously incorrect messages to be included in any school curriculum as they strike at core values needed not only in childhood, but in adulthood as well. We need faithful partners and we need the police to protect us from those intending harm.

I think there are endless ways we could inspire an eight-year-old to read without it involving an immoral husband. I think middle schoolers could be asked to write about how they contribute to society instead of reading a victim narrative targeting those tasked with enforcing the law.

And yes, some men cheat on their wives. And some wives cheat on their husbands. Not all police officers do justice to the badge they wear. Some parents belong in jail. And some adults have no common sense and act like idiots. These are facts of life. These "facts" however, do not apply to the majority so do not, in my opinion, belong in any school curriculum.

Our children should be educated so they have excellent academic skills that allow them to succeed. This includes getting students able to think and act for themselves, making their own decisions, and coming to their own conclusions about social issues and life.

The Extra-Credit, Community Service Hours and Grading Fraud

As if the materials used in modern schools are not horrific enough, the grading systems used in schools do not reflect the actual skill of a student. Report cards cannot be relied upon to be an accurate indication of a student's true skill. (This is obvious when we see students earning high school diplomas who cannot read above a third-grade level.)

It used to be that in order to receive an **A** one had to score 90 to 100 percent on the majority of assignments. A **B** grade would be issued for work that averaged 80 to 89 percent. Grades were issued based on the work the student completed, with each assignment earning a percent. In other words, the letter grades **A**, **B**, **C**, **D** and **F** posted on a quarterly report card were the average of all the scores (percentages of correct answers) for that time period. This is no longer the case.

Doing "extra-credit" to raise a grade is nothing new. This used to mean that a student would have to do extra math assignments or write an additional report. Many times, the "extra-credit" work was far more intense than the original assignments. This was to teach the student to do the work correctly the first time.

"Extra-credit" no longer requires extra work. Extra-credit can be earned by the student simply donating dry erase markers to the teacher. Office supplies can take a **C** to a **B** or even an **A** depending on the item(s) donated. (I am not making this up.)

Further, the classification of receiving a percentage on an assignment no longer reflects what the student got correct. In the old days, if one got a 95 percent on a quiz, they knew the material fairly well. Today a percentage shows how much of the assignment 'was completed,' with no emphasis on what was actually understood.

Let's say a student turns in a math lesson of 50 multiplication problems. As the student wrote answers for all 50 problems, he or she would receive 100 percent, even if none of the answers were correct. The student is not graded on what they actually know.

Parents are all too happy with a good report card but do not "see" that the grades are false, and their child cannot read, write or do grade level math. When I look at one of these report cards, I know with certainty that the document cannot be trusted.

In Florida, students are required to perform a minimum of 75 hours of community service to graduate. Instead of actually volunteering to help out a non-profit, students can be awarded community service hours by donating goods. Donate a $7 case of water following a hurricane and one can earn 50 community service hours.

Besides being a complete fraud (which one of us wants to get a tooth removed by a dentist who did not honestly earn a high school diploma?), this instills in our youth that they do not have to work for anything. No wonder our teenagers are so disconnected.

These are not isolated incidents of one or two kids. This is widespread in my community. If this is happening in the public, private and charter schools in Miami, it is safe to say it is happening nationwide.

My lower school teachers have encountered children in the fourth, fifth and sixth grades who all had nice report cards, passing to the next grade, yet could not read the sentence, "The pig is in the mud." (Not an exaggeration). The grades on the report cards are absolutely meaningless. When asking parents how the child progressed in grades without any skills, the parents said that their child earned "homework passes" and "grade forgiveness" for donating school supplies to the class.

I have run into middle and high school students who are of the mindset that if they have a failing grade, they fix it by getting their parents to donate paper towels.

One memorable example was after enrolling a high school student who transferred from a very well-known local private school. The student received an **F** in English because she did not do the assignments. The mother of said student came into my office with checkbook in hand asking how much she would need to donate to raise the grade. She explained that her daughter was planning to go to college and the **F** would "ruin her transcript," affecting scholarship opportunities. As the previous school accepted donations for "report card help" the mother was asking me to name my price. (Actually, she wanted me to change the English grade and add an entire high school math credit of a class her daughter never took, and based on existing skills, never would have passed.)

What an example this woman was setting for her daughter!

I was not interested in her money. I explained to this woman, as if I was talking to a two-year-old, that her daughter (like all students) actually needed to work to earn a higher grade. In this case, the girl would have to do an eight-week summer class with assignments done well to bring her English grade up. In terms of a missing math credit, these typically take a full school year to earn.

The mother did not like what I was saying so withdrew her child from my school opting, I assume, to go to a school where students did not have to complete assignments and bribes were accepted in exchange for diplomas.

Huang · Charter School Student

Huang was a seventh grader practically ready for med school. Really smart. He attended a charter school and though only 12 years old, he was taking high school advanced math classes. His parents hired me to help Huang with essays and reports. His first language was Chinese, so he needed assistance expressing his thoughts in English on paper.

Huang came in announcing: "*I have an assignment that you are absolutely going to hate.*"

Me: "*Tell me.*"

Huang: "*I need to write three paragraphs about World War II, but I am only allowed to use a website approved by the school.*"

Me: "*I do hate it. No one should tell you where and how to research, but let's look at the website before I decide I am outraged.*"

The website's article about WW II was about five paragraphs long. The first six words: "*Hitler was a very bad man.*" And that was all that was written about Hitler. No mention of the Holocaust, the victims, or the Nazis.

The article made it seem like someone in Germany got greedy, started stealing property and things got out of hand.

Me: *"Huang, this here wins for worst article ever written. The world did not go to war because someone in Germany stole a few paintings or bounced a check. We are going elsewhere for information."*

I explained that "a bad man" is someone who steals bikes or robs banks. When I told Huang that Hitler was responsible for the murder of 10 million people he deemed "unworthy of life" or "useless eaters," Huang could not believe it.

Huang: *"This really happened? He used those words?"*

Me: *"Yes."*

We then did our own research using the internet and books from school, writing a proper paper (not something based on a watered-down, history-changing version "approved" by the educational authorities). Huang chose his WW II topic, cited his sources, and included a few photos we printed.

I included a handwritten note to Huang's teacher, explaining that I found the "state approved website" inadequate, adding that I wanted Huang to receive a grade that reflected his work; otherwise, I'd be stopping by for a chat. He received a much-deserved A+.

Tommy, First Grade · Public School Student

Tommy was six years old and on the autism spectrum when he came to me for tutoring. His mother came to see me privately, stating her son was a sweetheart but he flapped his hands when he got excited and sometimes would talk so fast he stumbled over his words. He liked school but was frustrated as he was failing math. He had been extensively tested and evaluated with an existing IEP (Individual Educational Plan) that outlined special learning accommodations.

The mother wanted me to tutor Tommy twice a week on math.

As is typical with all younger children I tutor, I ask the parent what cartoon or animal their child likes so I either print coloring pages or purchase stickers to be used as rewards in our tutoring sessions. Here is how this went:

Me: "*What does Tommy like? Batman? Superman? Sharks? I am going to buy some stickers to use as rewards.*"

Mom: "*Tommy loves anything Toy Story. He also likes dinosaurs. But please do not get him dinosaurs or Toy Story things. Tommy's therapist says Tommy could develop OCD* [Obsessive-Compulsive Disorder] *if I give into his interests.*" (Word for word what she said!)

Me: "*That is the dumbest thing I have heard of.*"

Mom: "*I am just telling you what the therapist says. Maybe you can get Tommy something to do with cars or trains.*"

Me: "*No. I am going to work with Tommy offering rewards on things he likes. If the therapist has a problem with me giving Tommy dinosaur or Toy Story stickers, I'll give Tommy stickers of Rex, the dinosaur from Toy Story. The therapist should come by. I'd really like to meet her.*"

Mom: "*I'll tell her to schedule an appointment. It would be wonderful if we were all coordinated.*"

The meeting never occurred.

I was told that Tommy received three homework packets per week (reading, language, and math). I only became familiar with the math homework. Each math packet contained 20 worksheets, requiring the student to complete four pages each night for homework. Each page had 20 to 25 math problems, meaning Tommy had to do 80 to 100 individual math problems every single night. The font size of the math pack was size 8, making the problems very small and difficult to read. (Remember, this was only math. He had reading and language homework as well.)

Besides the problem of expecting this six-year-old autistic boy to remain seated for hours after school which violates common sense, the skill set contained in the math packets was way beyond first grade.

Tommy was supposed to add and subtract triple-digit numbers, identify time and money. There were fractions and long division. The word problems required several steps to solve. Isn't the point of diagnosing a child with special needs to come up with a plan to address those needs? This would have been a challenge for a fifth grader, let alone a six-year-old boy diagnosed with autism.

The day after I met with Tommy's mother and received his math packet, Tommy arrived for his first tutoring session. Blonde with a smile from ear to ear. He shook my hand. I showed him my stack of Toy Story coloring pages and dinosaur stickers, then we got down to the business of math. I held up three fingers.

Me: *"How many fingers am I holding up?"*

Tommy: *"Nine!"*

Me: *"Let's count. One... Two... Three... Good."*

"How many fingers am I holding up?"

Tommy: *"Two!"*

In under five seconds, I determined that Tommy could not count. I did not need an IEP. I did not need a fancy test. I did not need a checklist or degree.

(How did his teacher—a certified autism specialist—miss this? Did she really think giving this boy 80 problems of sixth grade level math a night was going to help him advance? Is that what she learned in college? In my opinion, this teacher was completely incompetent. In my opinion, her "certification" was useless.)

Starting with four identical wood blocks, I asked Tommy to count them as he touched them. He'd touch the first block and say, *"One, two, three..."* Then the next block, *"Four, five...."* and so on. He was saying multiple numbers for each object he touched. There were only four blocks on my desk, but he "counted" eleven.

Guiding his hand and his counting, I took him around the school, making him touch, then say, counting numbers up to ten with me. We counted tables, chairs, computers, paper cups, books, and crayons. We went outside, counting while touching benches, trees, windows, people, shopping carts, leaves, and so on.

At the end of each tutoring session, Tommy got stickers and coloring sheets of whatever he wanted. He loved his time with me. And I felt the same about him.

He did flap his hands when he got excited, and he did sometimes have so much to say that he would not be able to keep up with his words. Without any coaching from me, he tried to self-correct his speech. I patiently waited for him to finish forming an idea and patiently waited for the words to come out. I did not snap at him.

Long story short, it took me three hours to teach Tommy to count objects up to ten. This was three hours well spent. In 10 hours of tutoring, Tommy learned how to hold a pencil properly, write digits 0 to 9, and count to ten. It was a start.

He learned several games, which on the surface may not seem like much, but in reality it was exactly what he needed. He learned to take turns, follow directions, roll dice, move game pieces, and count spaces. He won games. He lost games without personal upset.

He could learn when given material that was learnable and at his level. I am not an autism specialist, but I think I made more progress with Tommy in ten hours of tutoring than he made in two years of special classes surrounded by "experts" in public school. He followed directions and took pride when he improved. He was honest, sincere and nothing but a joy.

Tommy needed what all six-year-old boys need. He needed to be loved and admired for exactly who he was. He needed to be shown how to make up his bed and where his shoes go. He needed to help cook dinner and be told that the sauce he stirred or the carrots he cut made the meal taste even better.

He needed dinosaur pajamas and to be tucked in at night. He needed to be read a story. He needed a goldfish or a hamster or maybe even a dog. He needed to build tents out of blankets and put together puzzles and work with LEGO bricks. He needed to be told "he could do anything, be anything."

He did not need a therapist to question his choice of favorite cartoon. He did not need an autism specialist to ignore his actual skills, robotically giving him the same work everyone else received. I thought the whole point of labeling him "special needs" was so that these needs were addressed.

Unfortunately for Tommy, his therapist advised the mother to discontinue tutoring. Tommy needed tutoring for first grade and only first grade. Having him work on pre-school skills (what I was doing) was considered by the therapist a waste of time and money.

Maria, Grade Five · Public Elementary School

Maria was ten when I began tutoring her. She had two brothers, both in their 20s. Maria's mother, an older woman, told me that God sent Maria as a blessing. Being the only girl of a Cuban family, Maria was raised with a lot of attention and care. Her family just adored her.

Impeccably dressed, head to toe, in "Hello Kitty" right down to shoelaces and hair ties. She had pets, liked to sing, was active in Sunday School and said her prayers nightly. If ever there was an argument for cloning, this little girl is the one to be cloned.

I was asked to tutor her as neither parent spoke English well enough to help her with homework.

I asked Maria what she wanted help with the most and she said math was her worst subject. She consistently got "**D**s." Within seconds of opening her Common Core textbook, it was crystal clear why Maria struggled in math. One page was addition, the next was dividing decimals and the next was pre-algebra with multiplication. (Remember, Maria was only a ten-year-old!) No mastery of skills. No logic. No gradient approach. One just threw together random pages of math, bound it, and called it a textbook.

Next are two examples of math problems from Maria's fifth grade *Go Math Workbook*.

Page 14

Use subtraction.

```
8 x 59  =  8 x ( ____ - 1 )

        = ( ____ x 60) - (8 x ____ )

        = ____ - ____

        = ____
```

How about just teaching Maria how to multiply 8 x 59?

Page 16

Test Prep

Canoes rent for \$29 per day. Which expression can be used to find the cost in dollars of renting 6 canoes for a day?

A) (6 + 20) + (6 + 9)

B) (6 X 20) + (6 X 9)

C) (6 + 20) X (6 + 9)

D) (6 X 20) X (6 X 9)

How about just having Maria figure out 6 x \$29?

My definition of a logical sequence is one must be able to walk before they can run; one learns letter sounds before they read words, and so on.

Chapter 1 of her math textbook included addition, making change (subtracting with money), division, fractions, word problems, multiplication and five other math concepts that are typically learned for high school level math. None of the work was presented in any logical sequence. Maria was lost. She was essentially expected to do a backflip on a balance beam before she could stand on one foot.

There is a simple approach to learning math that works and can be taught. But it is not what is being used in schools today.

The only possible use for the *Go Math* books would be to round all the books up and donate them to local firefighters to set on fire and use for drills. Seriously. The entire series of books should be discarded.

It took me about three hours to sort Maria's math out. I used old D. C. Heath Math textbooks from the 1980s. Are the books perfect? Not even close. But they are 100 times better than what Maria was using.

Grammar, language and reading lessons and texts assigned to Maria were similar to *Go Math* and likewise useless. I handled Maria's confusions in these subjects using older, out of print books. I was doing what the school system should have been doing. If the school system was doing their job, Maria would not have needed tutoring.

Then came the day Maria brought me a science packet. Four printed pages with information and a question and answer section. She was studying the human body. The packet was about sexually transmitted diseases, requiring her to draw male genitalia as it would look with and without herpes. There was a photograph (not a drawing) of a man's private parts to use as a guide.

Are you kidding me? This little princess of a girl was assigned to draw a penis for science homework.

Not happening.

I refused to have her read or do any of her science homework. I stapled a blank cover sheet over the packet and wrote the teacher a note voicing my outrage, stating I was willing to stop by for a chat. Maria's mother agreed with my stance.

From the Department of Justice website: *Federal law strictly prohibits the distribution of obscene matter to minors. Any transfer or attempt to transfer such material to a minor under the age of 16, including over the Internet, is punishable under federal law.*

The assignment is an example of "obscenity" being passed on as "science." This girl (or any fifth grader for that matter) has no business entering the world of sexually transmitted diseases.

The school could have done a lesson on skeletons, requiring the students to build little skeletons out of Q-tips. They could have done a lesson on DNA, asking each child to bring photos of the parents and grandparents when they were in fifth grade to compare differences and similarities. There are about a thousand lessons one could teach about the human body without requiring a ten-year-old to draw a penis infected with herpes.

Kenny

Kenny's parents came to me seeking help for their son. Kenny did not do his phonics homework or a Spanish Heritage coloring page. He also refused to hold a crayon properly. The school director wanted to schedule Kenny for a series of evaluations as he showed signs of learning disorders.

Fact: Kenny was 18 months old.

He was a baby!

Not yet two years old.

Here is the other fact: Some boxes of crayons state "not recommended for children under three." So, if we are being honest, Kenny should not have been being coached on how to hold a crayon as he was only one and a half years old.

I don't think we need to do a million-dollar research study to know what any toddler will do with a crayon: They are going to try to eat it.

I call this practice of giving a toddler schoolwork "dumb." Educators and "experts" call it "Early Intervention."

The practice leads parents to think that putting their child into an Early Intervention program will somehow make the child "be ahead of the game."

Trying to teach a baby to write is, on the surface, ridiculous, but taking a deeper view, this practice puts the child at a severe disadvantage by demanding of the child abilities he does not yet possess. He will learn to write, he will drive, and he will learn to balance a checkbook. Just not right now. Force him to write when his fingers are not developed, and he will accumulate losses and may grow to hate writing.

And let's not forget: Kenny was still in diapers.

The best way I know to help a child improve and learn new skills is to let them grow up in a safe, loving environment. Read to them before bed, provide them toys at bath time, go for walks, let them help with dusting or washing a car. Invest in LEGO bricks or building blocks. These (and similar activities) cultivate a sense of worth in the child, while getting him or her better able to control their bodies, control their environment and control their time.

Hinting a baby may be "delayed" over not doing homework should raise red flags for any parent. One should ask what is really going on? Is the director participating in a "research study" that needs warm bodies to experiment on? Is the director getting compensated?

The director in this case was all too ready to start a screening process which would lead to labels, which would lead to therapy, which would lead to medication. Does she really think this boy's quality of life is going to suffer because the parents did not give him crayons at 18 months?

Speaking of homework, these are the actual scans of the phonics assignments Kenny was supposed to do. Anyone who has made a black-and-white copy from a color page knows that the image comes out black. In the first image, the student is supposed to trace the letters "Cc," and with the second image, they are supposed to count the objects in the tree, drawing a circle around the correct number of items found.

Let's pretend for a minute that Kenny was not a year old. Let's say he was five. How about we show some respect to the student and respect to the field of education by giving him a worksheet that is clear and not black.

Let's not forget that this little boy is a client of the school. His parents are paying for a service. If we are going to give a toddler an assignment (that he will put in his mouth) shouldn't it at least be legible?

Would the teacher who issued this packet be satisfied if her daughter's wedding invitations were of the same quality? Would she pay for graduation announcements for her son that looked like the above? What "rating scale" would this earn? How many other low-quality packets does this school hand out?

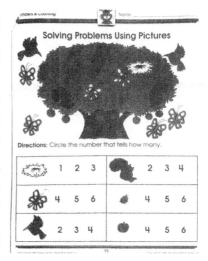

And if I really want to get picky (which you know I do), this is copyrighted material and illegal to reproduce in a school setting without proper licensing.

We need to hold our educators to a much higher standard. The bar is already set so terribly low.

Chapter 10

A Word About Electronic Devices

I think my generation was the last to make forts out of fallen branches, play hide and seek on summer nights, and read books as the main forms of entertainment. My own children were raised playing outside, climbing trees, feeding birds, running in the rain, turning large boxes into clubhouses, setting up backyard tents, baking cookies, collecting bugs, and doing all the things kids should do. I could tell it was an especially good day by how dirty they were at bath time.

I believe that the influence and broad adoption of devices (cell phones, video games, tablets) over the last 30 years has negatively impacted the learning process, thus, childhood. Now, instead of using a bucket of building blocks to make a structure, one can design one on a device. I have students who spend a minimum of eight hours a day on video games. This time increases on weekends, with kids doing nothing else but playing on a device. Mathematically, eight hours a day works out to 2,920 hours per year. As many kids start using devices around the age of two, this works out to 29,200 hours in front of a screen for an average 12-year-old kid. If this same child had spent half that time playing sports, drawing, learning to sew, writing stories, or reading books, I guarantee that child would be better equipped academically. And better prepared for adulthood.

I cannot tell you how many parent meetings I have had where the child in question has low grades, showing up to school with insufficient hours of sleep because they were up half the night using a device. The "outraged" parent usually says something like, "All my son/daughter wants to do is play Xbox. What can I do?"

This is a no-brainer. Don't buy an Xbox! Remove the TV from the bedroom, disconnect the Xbox, put it in the trunk of your car and don't buy any more games. The kids did not buy the video games, the parent did. The reason parents put devices in front of their children to begin with is so that they, the parents, do not have to deal with their kid(s). The device becomes a convenient babysitter.

This is a general statement, but I have found that most kids who were permitted to spend hours in front of a screen did not like to read, were behind in math and/or had poor life skills (did not know how to use a broom or wash dishes). I also find many of these kids unaware of how to behave in social situations as they have not been taught basic communication skills of eye contact and saying "please" and "thank you."

Based on my experience working with children, the ones dependent on (addicted to) devices tend to move slower, think slower, get tired easily and cannot solve even the smallest of life's problems, such as what to do when their pencil breaks. (Seriously, one 11-year-old boy just held his broken pencil up waiting for me to give directions on what to do.)

Once a child is addicted to devices, it is very hard to get them "un-addicted."

It is sad to enter a restaurant and see a family glued to their phones and not engaging with each other. And don't get me started on toddlers with game devices affixed to their strollers. Today's automobiles are equipped with monitors. Heaven forbid parents actually carry on a conversation with their child, even if it is: *"Look at the cows."* or *"Check out the Christmas lights!"*

I have encountered ten-year-olds who have never played a board game, rolled dice, or used their fingers to move a game piece. Once they understand the game, these kids really enjoy the experience. One can see their ability to think strategically develop.

I have encountered teenagers who never helped cook a meal and several who never sat down to dinner as a family. One teenaged boy had a vitamin D deficiency due to the fact he never played outdoors. Never is a strong word but applies in this case. The boy was about four grade levels behind, parents insisted he had learning disabilities, yet the boy had no issue recalling the time and day of the full prime-time TV line-up of all his favorite shows.

Last hurricane, parts of Miami were without power for days. Children and adults practically lost their minds. They did not know what to do with themselves. That is how dependent our society today has become on devices.

To add to this problem, in Miami there are schools that are 100 percent computer based. Children are herded into classrooms and sit in front of a screen for every subject without any human interaction. Or children are taught at home via an on-line platform. This is just depressing. It is one thing for an adult to take on-line classes, but I personally am 100 percent opposed to this activity for children.

There are several on-line public school reading programs that flash words at a student, which is somehow supposed to get them reading. There is no option to ask questions or voice an opinion. There is no interaction with a living, breathing teacher. Words and sentences just continue to flash at the student reminding me of some type of rapid hypnosis. It is disturbing. (100 percent of the students and parents I have spoken to who were using such a program hate it—that alone should tell one how effective it is.)

Education is, in its simplest form, a communication process with the best teachers being the ones with the best communication skills.

Many times, I have invited my children to help me in the kitchen, showing them how to make cookies. They took turns cracking eggs, adding sugar, and stirring the batter. Things would get spilled, and things would get cleaned up. Questions were asked; answers were given. This simple experience, and many more like it, is what learning is about. Whether one is baking a cake or learning about fractions, in my opinion, it is best done human to human.

Technology in the form of phones, devices, computer learning programs should never take the place of the human experience. To do so robs the child and the teacher of an emotional, often spiritual, connection that occurs when true learning takes place.

Technology is a tool. It should never become a substitute for human interaction. Technology that results in making someone lazy or less active should not be used in educating children. I am not saying we all need to return to wearing prairie dresses and braids. I am saying that when we allow "technology" to replace the human experience, we all lose.

Chapter 11

Stories (Getting it Wrong)

Pedro

Pedro was a 16-year-old boy who was struggling in 11th grade classes at a local public school. His parents wanted him to get a standard high school diploma and thought a smaller school setting would benefit him as he needed more attention.

The family arrived for the enrollment interview at my school with a folder an inch thick, containing all the evaluations dating back to pre-kindergarten that determined him to have "unspecified learning disorders." Pedro was currently taking mainstream classes with weekly accommodations (meaning a tutor would come in twice a week to help him with his work).

Despite being passed to 11th grade by a local public high school, Pedro's actual skills were around a second-grade level. He could not add, subtract, multiply or divide. He could not accurately tell time or identify money. He could not write a paragraph or read beginner chapter books (longer stories broken down into short sections) and did not know how to spell very well.

Clearly drugged, I asked him his name. He thought about it, blinked slowly a few times before telling me. Took about seven full seconds. I then held up a yellow crayon, asking him to tell me its color. Again, he had to think about it. Look it over. Concentrate. Focus. About seven full seconds later, he correctly told me the crayon was yellow. At this pace, considering the skill level required to earn a standard diploma, it would take another 20 years of school for Pedro to get there.

His parents explained that he was prescribed ADHD medication at age four and had been on one or more medications ever since.

This boy was just two years shy of being considered a legal adult and was, in my opinion, catatonic due to the drugs in his system. He behaved like a slow robot. He spoke like a robot.

A seven-second reaction time makes his employment options almost non-existent, denying him any hope of adult independence. Paying rent, shopping for groceries, forming adult relationships, and managing money require a faster reaction time.

Then there is the fact that this boy becomes a danger the minute he gets behind the wheel of a car, as he may slam on his brakes seven seconds too late. I bring this up as, unfortunately, in his case, his parents recently bought him a brand new car for his sixteenth birthday.

The parents were part of the problem. They did not actually see their son. They were focused on his age, not his ability. He had no business riding a bike, much less driving a car as he was unaware of his surroundings. He was probably unaware he had a nose.

I did not accept Pedro for school enrollment as neither he nor his parents were interested in catching him up. They simply wanted him to graduate on time with a diploma and I could not guarantee this would occur.

Amy

Amy was a new student enrolling for ninth grade. She had been labeled with multiple learning disabilities and had been on multiple medications throughout her life. Despite all the ADHD medications and "academic therapies" by the hands of psychologists, TerraNova standardized tests placed her at a high second-grade level in math and a fourth-grade level in reading and language. In other words, she was between five and seven grades behind.

In math, it was quickly discovered that Amy never mastered adding and subtracting. Though 14, she had to count on her fingers to add "5 plus 3." She could not count by 2's. Her previous school allowed her to use a calculator beginning in third grade. We do not permit calculators, so Amy had to learn math, starting with simple addition.

H.E.L.P. Miami (my school) typically does not assign much, if any, homework; however, Amy had a tremendous amount of math to master if we had any hope of graduating her on time with a standard diploma. We gave her three worksheets of simple addition to practice.

She came in the following day with only seven or eight problems done. Her mother said Amy felt "depressed" over being so far behind so was not motivated to do the work.

I explained that the only way Amy could catch up was to learn the skills required for high school. The only way to catch up was to do the work.

I suggested Amy drill flash cards with her mom for 30 minutes each night. This was not done; per the mom it was too stressful. Mom explained that Amy could not process things the way others did and got overwhelmed easily.

Not surprisingly, I learned that Amy was not given chores at home or expected to do much of anything. She spent hours in front of the TV, on her phone or playing video games, all while her mother "coddled" and "pampered" her "educational/social anxiety."

A month into the school year, Amy began showing up later and later. After showing up two hours late, I told Amy she needed to be on time or she would be dismissed from my school. I explained that high school is a warm-up for the real world; explained that the REAL WORLD runs on deadlines and is very stressful for those who are not prepared.

Her mother came to me very upset, stating that I was not accommodating Amy's special needs. Her daughter needed "sympathy and understanding," not "forceful" direction or "threats of dismissal." Here is how that conversation went:

Amy's mother: "*Amy's psychologist is shocked that you are demanding she show up on time and are ignoring the fact that Amy suffers from a 'Scheduling Disorder.'*"

Me: "*I have never heard of 'Scheduling Disorder.' I don't think that is a thing.*"

Mother: "*It is a disorder. Amy's brain cannot process time.*" (In the meantime, Amy plays multiple video games that require tasks get completed in a set amount of time and she never missed her favorite TV show.)

Me: "*She will have to learn to process time.*"

Mother: "*You are being offensive and unreasonable.*"

Me: "*Fair enough. I will need a note from a qualified medical doctor stating that Amy will experience organ failure or her health will be put at risk if she has to show up to school on time. Unless I get the note, she has to be in her seat like everyone else at 9:00 in the morning. Her school assignments will have to be completed when due, otherwise she will not pass. So please bring me a note. I'd also like the doctor to provide the blood test, CAT scan or medical test results that determine she suffers from 'Scheduling Disorder.'*"

The mother withdrew Amy from school.

I stand by my view. Today it is "scheduling disorder," tomorrow it will be "lost sock in dryer emotional disorder" and next week it will be "can't get a job disorder."

Life has its obligations. The most successful people I know have an abundance of obligations. Jobs, medical appointments, bus schedules, and bills all run on deadlines, schedules, and timetables.

In my opinion, parents who coddle, who pamper, who never say "no," who justify/defend bad behavior instead of correcting it, are responsible for ensuring that their child grows up "a delicate victim" or a "poorly mannered jerk" and stays that way. Between the way this girl was being raised at home and the family psychologist's insistence that "she will never be able to do anything on time," this girl does not stand a chance. Shame on both the mother and the family psychologist for providing a "mental illness" that will prevent this otherwise normal teenager from properly growing up.

Danny

Danny was ten years old and in the fifth grade when he came to me for tutoring. His reading and math were at a kindergarten level based on a quick assessment that I did, not an official test. (I asked him to read a first-grade level book out loud and I gave him simple arithmetic problems to solve. He could not read the book and he did not correctly solve the math problems.)

In addition to Danny being passed through grades without knowing the material, Danny's parents found out that since kindergarten, Danny had been getting mental health treatment at school. The parents were rightfully outraged as they had no idea that their son was receiving "therapy." They found out when Danny came home asking to be put on "learning drugs" like his friends were taking.

When the parents confronted the school administration on their lack of consent for therapy, the school responded that the parents did give their consent by signing an Emergency Medical Release. This release is standard within the education system. If a child breaks their arm in school and the parents cannot be reached, the release allows the school to "treat" the child by calling an ambulance, performing CPR, or otherwise administering first aid. The school administration extended the Medical Release to include giving psychiatric treatment to Danny. Upon getting information about the "treatment" their son was receiving, the parents found that Danny was told he had 18 learning and behavioral disorders, convincing Danny that he was unable to learn.

The parents were furious that their son had been getting "ADHD therapy" without their knowledge. It was at this time that they found an attorney and sought me out to tutor their son.

The biggest barrier to helping Danny was getting over his fixed idea that he was "learning disabled." He firmly believed that he could not learn. I addressed this by asking him a series of questions, such as: Who dressed you today? Who tied your shoes? Who held the toothbrush when you brushed your teeth? Once it was firmly established that Danny was successfully potty trained, could dress himself, learned to play sports, and spoke two languages, he agreed that he could learn easy things but remained convinced he would never learn "the hard stuff."

Besides the lack of knowledge of letter sounds and the inability to do simple addition and subtraction, Danny's handwriting was horrendous. He did not know why writing legibly was important. He had never been taught the correct sequence to form letters and numbers. He looked at a letter or a number and did his best to write it.

Not surprisingly, sloppy handwriting is an indication of "learning disability or mental health issue" per multiple Teacher Rating checklists.

His parents were ready to take Danny out of baseball so he could work with me five days a week. I suggested they keep him in baseball. He liked being part of a team. I felt taking him out would act as a punishment and only make him worse. They kept him in baseball, scheduling tutoring three times a week.

My approach was simple. First of all, I did not try to fix his entire education in an hour. The one-hour tutoring sessions would go like this: the first ten minutes was spent following directions by putting together a LEGO car, motorcycle, etc. (LEGO sets have booklets that show step-by-step how to build something.) I would spend 15 to 20 minutes practicing alphabet letter sounds, choosing a couple of letters for Danny to form using Play-Doh. I would read to Danny, using beginner reader books, having him read sections that I knew he could. Then we'd do a few math problems and play a game. Danny got stickers for good penmanship and for doing work.

Danny was very easy to work with and he looked forward to tutoring. I made it fun. Within the school year, Danny made drastic improvement in reading and math. Even his teachers noticed the difference.

The parents filed a lawsuit against the school for giving their son six years of psychiatric therapy without consent. I was called as an "expert witness" on Danny's behalf. I was told by legal counsel that I would be "ripped apart" by the opposing lawyer and to not take it personally.

The proceedings were to occur over a two-day timeline. Day one, the public school would state their case; day two, witnesses for Danny would state theirs. As it turns out, the public school took three days. I have no idea what was said, as I was not permitted in the courtroom. I just know that Danny's mother was on the verge of a meltdown. To add to the tension, CNN was there with a camera.

Day four came and Danny's case was falling apart. Two key witnesses were denied testimony due to an error in court procedure. This left me as the only person to speak on Danny's behalf.

I entered the courtroom and took the stand noticing that the right side of the courtroom had 20 or so Miami-Dade public school officials sitting behind a very put-together lawyer, full of confidence, who looked like he just stepped out of a magazine. This was the man who was going to discredit me piece by piece.

On the left side of the courtroom were Danny's stressed parents, sitting behind a disheveled, relatively new attorney in a suit that did not properly fit.

First question from Danny's attorney: "*What credentials do you have as an educator?*"

"*None.*"

What degrees? "*None.*" What certificates? "*None.*" Do you consider yourself an educator? "*Professionally, no. Non-professionally, yes.*"

I explained that I homeschooled my four children. I held up their birth certificates and homeschool documentation with student identification numbers from the county.

I was questioned about the materials I used to tutor Danny.

I showed the court Danny's phonics workbook and math worksheets he had completed and the ones he was working on. I outlined a typical tutoring session. I was asked about Danny's ADHD.

"*I am not a psychologist so cannot speak to that. I can say that when Danny works with me, he is focused and has no problem completing the assigned tasks.*"

I was asked what method of therapy I used to keep Danny motivated.

"*I am not a therapist. I am a homeschooler. I use stickers to keep him motivated. He likes dinosaurs and Batman.*"

I was asked if Danny ever said he wanted to play baseball instead of do homework.

"*No. Danny has never asked to play baseball when working with me.*"

I asked if I could say more. The judge allowed it.

"*I am not surprised Danny would rather play baseball than do three hours of homework. He is a ten-year-old boy. I have three boys; they'd all prefer to play than do schoolwork. None of them have ever asked for math books for Christmas and if they did, I'd be worried."*

The judge laughed.

I was asked about Danny's hyper behavior at home and at school, as a sign of ADHD.

"I am not a psychologist, so cannot speak about ADHD. Danny works with me at a table, and I do not see anything I would call 'hyper.'"

I asked if I could elaborate. The judge allowed it.

"I have a problem calling any child 'hyper.' What exactly does that mean? Hyper compared to what? Adults? My parents did not get matching furniture until all five of their children moved out of the house. We were constantly moving, playing indoor tag, jumping over the sofa on the way to the kitchen and so on. My parents only became concerned when things were calm and quiet. I think Danny is just a normal ten-year-old boy."

I was on the stand for 45 minutes. I am sure I appeared calm, but I was anything but. My heart was beating out of my chest. I was the only educator permitted to testify on Danny's behalf and I wasn't "certified."

Now it was time for opposing counsel to question me. I internally braced myself for what was coming.

He stood up, locked eyes with me and told the judge he had no questions for me.

I left him nothing to challenge. Nothing to doubt. Nothing to say. The judge thanked me for my testimony and asked me to leave.

Danny's parents ended up winning their case. Danny's "school therapy" was discontinued and I believe his labels were canceled, pending a new set of evaluations.

Educational whistleblower and best-selling author, Beverly Eakman, followed this story closely, interviewing both parents and myself outside of the courtroom. Her published article entitled "Uncle Sam's Classroom" fully documents how Danny was targeted by "mental health experts" in public school. This article is contained in her book, *Walking Targets*.

"Uncle Sam's Classroom Excerpt" from *Walking Targets*, page 45:

Yolanda and Raul Salazar of Miami, Florida, naturalized citizens who escaped Castro's Cuba, found out the hard way that Uncle Sam's classrooms are not about proficiency at anything, or literacy, or basics. America's schools aren't extensions of the home, where families are held sacred and parents valued. Instead, American education is about "mental hygiene," defined by psychologists as "preventative psychotherapy."

I consider myself very lucky to have met Beverly. She was one of the warmest, most informed persons I have ever met.

Bella

Bella was a 14-year-old who transferred to H.E.L.P. Miami from a Florida boarding school for troubled teens that charged $7,000 per month.

Here is a portion of an email her mother received from the academic director that was passed on to me at the time of enrollment:

> Good Afternoon, Gladys,
> I just finished Bella's transcript.
> I provided her with an Algebra 1 credit, instead of remedial math. I did not want her to be behind....

The girl could barely do sixth grade math, yet the Academic Director gave her a full credit in Algebra so "she did not get behind." The Academic Director is, in my opinion, a fraud. He is not doing this girl any favors by giving her a high school credit in a class she did not take. I guess $7,000 monthly tuition paid for something, just not academic skills.

Unfortunately, this girl did not last two months in my school. She refused to do work and expected me to give her credits just for showing up.

Professional Child Therapist

Mary was a practicing child psychologist. She came to see me about her eight-year-old daughter and ten-year-old son. They were both on multiple meds (beginning in kindergarten) for ADHD, anxiety, behavior disorders and depression. Mary needed help as both children were failing school, and at home they were disrespectful and fought constantly.

After a short conversation, it was established that Mary was not willing to pay for tutoring (too much money), she was not going to change schools (may be too stressful for her kids), and she preferred to continue medicating her children as it was the "agreed-upon" protocol of her profession.

I was at a loss on why Mary would seek me out.

I pointed out that it would seem that the "agreed-upon protocols" of her profession were not resulting in better behaved, more intelligent, cooperative children.

She answered that she had no other choice but to medicate her children. That as a professional psychologist, she was bound by current standards outlined in the *DSM* (*Diagnostic and Statistical Manual of Mental Disorders*). It was a clear attempt to impress me with her "knowledge."

I gave her a history lesson.

I pointed out that one hundred years ago "the current standard" of the time did not allow women to vote. Four hundred years ago one could get beheaded for speaking out against a king, but "that's how things were done." Somewhere along the line one woman stood up, made a choice to go against society's fixed ideas so that women everywhere could benefit from her courage and be granted the right to vote. Somewhere along the line, some person made a choice to shake things up, to outlaw beheadings at the command of a king.

When people see something wrong, they can do something effective to fix it. One always has a choice. One can always be braver.

"How things are done" is not a justification for incompetence.

In my opinion, Mary was a professional coward.

How My Third Grade Teacher Tried to Shut Me Down

I loved school. I owned kindergarten, first and second grade. The teachers loved me, and I felt the same about them. If I made a gift for my mother or father, I'd make a gift for my teacher. I felt as if my teachers were part of my family.

Third grade was completely different. My teacher was a woman on the same bowling team as my mother, so she knew me. She was a big woman (think a female version of Jackie Gleason), loud, bossy, yelled at bowling pins when they did not fall, but up until I was her student, she had been nothing but kind to me in her loud, bossy way.

"Well, what'd you do with your front teeth? (More a statement than a question.) Did the Tooth Fairy leave you something? If she didn't just let me know, I have her number! (Her joke terrified me more than humored me. I mean, who threatens the Tooth Fairy?)

The class was mixed, third grade with fourth grade, and I was physically the smallest in the room. Terrible at sports. I was a slow runner and afraid of the ball, therefore, picked last for all playground games. However, I shined in the classroom as I always did.

In first grade, I'd draw pictures of words and my teacher would send me to other classes to show off my work. In second grade, I would make up poems with the spelling words and the teacher would have me read them in front of the class. I had earned several awards and made honor roll every quarter.

Third grade, however, was all business. Creativity took a back seat to academics. We watched the Watergate trial, for heaven's sake, for social studies. I thought I was the only one in the room clueless and bored out of my mind. I had no idea what was happening. (This was the first time in my life I was bored and confused at school.)

Music was another challenge. I have no talent or interest in singing. I was embarrassed to sing in front of the class. I knew I was terrible. But the teacher would bark, "Louder Barbara, louder!"

Enough Is Enough!

When it came to regular assignments, I was good. When I finished my work, I was allowed to quietly draw on my own.

At the time, there was a commercial that I really liked. It was a cartoon of a soda bottle turning into a 7UP® butterfly. The cartoon bottle was shadowed in such a way that it looked real to me. The art was true to the early seventies: it was "groovy." Whenever the commercial came on TV, I would try to notice something new. I wanted to mimic the style.

I was trying to work on shadowing, so it looked 3D. Once I figured out how to draw a decent soda bottle butterfly, I started to work on the background. I had mountains, flowers and each cloud was held up by helium balloons. In a few weeks, I must have drawn 100 different 7UP pictures during free time at school and at home. Finally, I was happy with the outcome: I had accomplished "groovy!" I was eight years old and felt my artwork was good enough to be featured on T.V.

Image from a 7UP commercial

My teacher had other ideas. On the first quarter report card, she gave me a **C** in art, a **C** in gym, and a **C** in music. Those were the first **C**'s I had ever received.

She told my mother that I did not sing loud enough.

In gym, she told my mother I used the fact that I had had heart surgery as an excuse not to participate. This was a lie. I had never had an adult lie about me before.

I had never thought of using my surgery to get out of anything. I don't think my parents would have tolerated me acting like that. I was never told to "be careful," nor was I prevented from riding bikes, climbing trees, or playing tag. One of the things I liked about my parents is that they did not limit me because I was a girl. If my brothers went fishing, so could I. If my brothers practiced shooting targets with a BB gun, then so could I. Other than an impressive scar, heart surgery was a non-issue.

The teacher told my mom that I got a **C** in art because I drew the same thing over and over again. I was limited in my ability. (I was being graded on drawings I did in my free time! Knife fully inserted in my back and twisted.)

My mother knew this would upset me. She actually told me that report cards aren't always important—a complete contradiction to what she told my older siblings. I cried for hours. Being the smallest and last picked for teams is not a confidence builder for anyone. Art was what set me apart from everyone else. Not bragging, but I was years ahead of third grade. I had, per my father, "a gift."

A gift that my earlier teachers fully recognized and encouraged.

When I entered second grade, our teacher asked us to draw something we did over summer. I drew a Florida beach. My drawing had the surf, sun, a sailboat in the distance, horseshoe crabs, sea shells, a sand castle, toys, a beach bag, clouds and three dolphin fins. The teacher (a lovely woman) called my mom to tell her how much detail I captured. The art was hung in the classroom with a gold star on it. My mother was in her eighties and still remembered getting that phone call about my beach drawing.

If my third grade teacher had asked me why I kept drawing a 7UP butterfly, she would have discovered I was not "limited," I was improving my skill. I was expanding my skill. I was working on shading. I wanted my butterfly to look 3D.

After Halloween, when the class started learning long division, I was stuck. I was confused. The teacher yelled at me in front of everyone: *"Don't get out of your seat until you figure it out! I have explained it enough!"*

Well, that's not a helpful attitude! I ended up shaking so badly I could not hold my pencil and then in front of everyone, I started to cry. And my teacher, Miss Flett, stood there glaring at me, as if staring me down made me smarter somehow.

Enough Is Enough!

I had never before encountered a teacher who spoke harshly to me. I had never encountered anything in school that I could not do until third grade.

A compassionate fellow third grader (without a formal teaching certificate) ended up helping me. His last name was Coffee, and I will not forget him walking me through, step by step, the process of long division until I could do it. Once I understood it, I was fine. But the emotional trauma of being in that class took its toll. I went from confident to worried.

Soon it was Christmas. My parents did not have money, but I would never have known it. Christmas was always exciting. I got Barbie Dolls, coloring books, stuffed animals, puzzles, and games. My Christmas stocking would be stuffed with fun little toys and treats.

I believed in Santa and had plans to stay awake all night so I could hear his sleigh. It was getting dark on Christmas Eve and, as was tradition, my parents told us all to hang our stockings before going to bed.

It was my father who noticed something was wrong. I did not follow my mom out of the room to find a sock I could use as a stocking, and I was on the verge of tears.

I told my dad that I was not going to hang a stocking as Santa wasn't going to bring me anything this year. I had been bad. I had not one, but three **C**s on my report card, and the teacher yelled at me about math.

My dad took me to his room, sat me on the bed and told me: *"Barbara, Santa looks at all your report cards, not just one. Right?"*

Me: *"Yes."*

Dad: *"You've had dozens and dozens of **A**s since kindergarten. Right?"*

Me: *"Yes."*

Dad: *"Santa knows how smart you are and knows you figured out long division. Santa also loves your art. He thinks you are very talented. One of the best he has ever seen."*

Me: (Too emotional to respond.)

Dad: "*Yes, sweetie. You're really, really good. Santa is not going to punish you at all. You are on the 'Good List.' There is one more thing though ... but you have to promise never to tell your mother.*"

Me: "*Okay.*"

Dad: "*Santa thinks your teacher is a moron.*"

And for the first time in months, I went to sleep with a happy heart.

And I am pretty sure my dad had just secured a place in heaven.

My father Jerry, with David and I

Chapter 12

Returning to My Questions

Going back to the beginning of this book, I had two questions that I was desperate to find the answer to.

I found my answer to both.

When Did School Start to Destroy the Child's Natural Ability to Learn?

This systematic takedown began well over 100 years ago by dismantling the most important academic skill, reading. This was followed by the degradation of math, language, and the other school subjects. These were ultimately replaced with propaganda aimed at keeping people dumb and unaware.

When declining academics became a nationwide concern, instead of going back to proven basics, the educational "experts" doubled down on psychological testing, checklists, evaluations, pharmaceuticals and other unproven/ineffective nonsense that turned normal behaviors into "childhood disorders." Such as the term "hyper-active." Children are not "hyper-active," they are naturally active.

This has made America the top prescriber of psychiatric medication for children.

The *DSM-5* (*Diagnostic and Statistical Manual of Mental Disorders, 5th Edition*) is the American Psychiatric Association's standard for identifying mental disorders. Disorders are not the same as a disease. A disease can be detected through blood, biopsies, scans and other objective measures. There is no scientific test to prove a disorder (a fact confirmed directly to my face by several child psychiatrists as covered in chapter 8) which seriously makes me question the validity of the *DSM* in general.

To further make my point, in 1973 the American Psychiatric Association considered homosexuality a mental disorder. Due to outrage by gay rights advocates, the APA Board of Directors voted to declassify being gay as a mental disorder, removing it from the *DSM-2*. If it was "voted out," it must have been "voted in" at an earlier point in time. This begs the question: how many other "disorders" were just voted into existence?

I, for one, would like to vote out cancer, but I don't think actual science works this way. I lost my father to cancer. Cancer is a real disease, detected by various physical tests. I was told my son had a "mental disorder" that prevented him from learning. This was false. Proven if only by the fact he had already learned two languages before he even started school.

The *DSM-5* is the industry standard of so-called disorders. It provides endless labels to fit every situation—if the child is confused at school, there is a label and a drug. If a child gets anxious before tests, there is a label and a drug. If a child is advanced, he is labeled "gifted" and put in an intense academic program designed to overwhelm, and when the child reaches his or her breaking point there is another label and a drug. If the child acts like a child, there is a label and a drug.

I personally have high standards. I pay attention to detail. I take pride in doing things well. I expect others to do things correctly. Per the *DSM-5*, I suffer from the psychiatric condition called OCD (Obsessive-Compulsive Disorder). Interesting that I am considered "mentally ill" for expecting my students to know their times tables perfectly, yet the aim of the educational experts running the show is only 70 percent accuracy for any given subject.

The field of education has further been hindered by dictionaries changing definitions of words to fit political and social agendas.

Parents are considered "domestic terrorists" for daring to challenge the sexually explicit material found in middle school library books.

Nationwide, schools banned the Pledge of Allegiance. Patriotism and pride are no longer taught.

God, faith, and any reference to the spiritual nature of man has been removed as a source of guidance and morality. There goes personal accountability, personal responsibility, self-control, and consequences for one's actions.

Enter the perpetually offended, the "coddle-mentality" and the birth of victimhood.

Nowadays, crime is not only tolerated, but also justified. Instead of disciplining a child, teachers are told to ignore them, making the school environment unstable and unsafe.

And there was my six-year-old boy, Damon, drowning in a system purposely designed to give him losses then shut him down with a label and drug. I cringe just thinking about it.

I also cringe when I see various posts of parents and grandparents happily sharing First Day of School photos. I see smiling children, fresh haircuts, cartoon lunchboxes and superhero backpacks.

I know with certainty that the child's excitement will soon turn to dread as their day-to-day life gets ruined by hours of mind-numbing seat work at school and then hours of stress-inducing homework at night. I know with certainty that some teacher "indoctrinated in college" will recommend screenings, evaluations, and tests. Then come the labels followed by multiple prescriptions (to find which drug combination works best).

I am confident in predicting that the once excited child will grow into a disconnected teenager who cannot write a proper sentence and has zero self-respect. A young adult who does not even know what it feels like not to be drugged. I see a teenager who is completely unaware of how unprepared for the world he or she actually is. And someone who is all too easy to manipulate and mold.

I did not want to lose my son to this.

And this leads me to my second question:

Where the Hell Was the 1990s Version of Anne Sullivan?

Where was the young woman who arrived on a train to tutor a blind, deaf, mute little girl named Helen? Where was the teacher who

Enough Is Enough!

became known as the Miracle Worker for successfully teaching Helen the meanings of words. Teaching Helen how to read. Teaching Helen how to communicate.

My son desperately needed to be rescued.

He needed a teacher who believed in him.

I found her.

For my son Damon, the rescuer, the teacher, was me.

Part Three

Chapter 13

Educational Options, Getting Started, and Advice

The only way to have complete control over your child's education is to step outside of traditional schooling and take all educational matters into your own hands.

If you find yourself fed up with your child's school or simply wanting a change, your options are:
- Enroll your child in a different school, realizing that if it is another "traditional school" you are likely to get the same psychological indoctrination, just packaged differently.
- Homeschool your child.
- Hire someone else to homeschool your child.
- Create a "micro-school" or a "learning pod" educating a small group of children. (This is what I did.)
- Enroll your child in a micro-school or learning pod.
- Start your own private school.

Note: I do not recommend online learning for children for reasons mentioned in previous chapters. Looking at a computer all day, even if there is a live person on the other end, is no substitute for the human connection. Despite their popularity, robots and computers will never take the place of face-to-face communication.

The other caution about homeschooling is that several states offer accredited or state-approved homeschooling curricula one can implement in their home. From my experience, this is the same ineffective material offered in school and should not be utilized.

The above options vary from state to state. Florida happens to be a very "homeschool" friendly state.

For those who think, "*I can't teach my kid,*" "*I have to work,*" or "*I have a career,*" I completely understand. I want to make it clear that home-schooling is no joke. It is not something one embarks upon lightly.

I personally did not think I was intelligent enough to teach my son. My parents had no faith in my ability to teach either: "*Barbara, what on earth are you talking about? You're not a teacher! Damon will be eating paint instead of learning to read!*"

In addition to doubting my teaching abilities, I had three other children under the age of four that, while very easy to manage, still demanded constant attention and interaction.

My apartment was small.

I had no idea of where to go for materials or even how to write a lesson plan.

I had every excuse for why homeschooling would not be workable.

I looked into enrolling Damon in a private school, but that was too expensive.

I looked into hiring a private tutor to work with Damon after school but could not afford that either. Plus, getting him "tutored" on materials I found deliberately difficult and confusing seemed to be a way of enhancing the problem, not solving it. Instead of giving him work at a level he could do, he'd just have been force-fed the same ineffective nonsense already being pushed. Even if I could have afforded it, after-school tutoring was not the answer.

In the meantime, I stood by watching my son slip away. He was no longer a vibrant, active boy. He had been robbed of his spirit. He was defeated. He factually thought he was stupid. Shut down; life over at age six.

This left me no choice but to take action. For me, homeschooling was not just a choice, it was a necessity. My son; my problem.

And it was time for me to stop being a spectator of the problem and actually do something productive about it.

Getting Started

The terms "micro-school" and "learning pod" did not exist when I started to homeschool in 1992, but essentially this is what I did. I felt my children would do better being homeschooled with children their same age.

Building a program around the age or grade of your child or children and taking on other children of the same age/grade is, in my opinion, the way to go. If your son or daughter is in third grade, you should find five other children of the same age or grade. This year you'd get them through third-grade material, next year you'd deliver fourth grade. This is much easier than taking on five children at five different grades (unless you personally have a family of five children needing five different grades).

You may need something that caters to a group of gymnasts. In this case, you may only want to accept gymnasts in your learning pod. You may want to create a Christian homeschool so would accept children of the same religion. However you structure your home-education program, if you have children, you should build the activity around *your* child's needs. This does not mean you show favoritism of any kind. It simply means that if you are determined to keep your six-year-old out of government run schools and you want them to have a few study-buddies, then find like-minded parents of six-year-olds and teach solely to that age group.

For my activity, parents interested in my services had to alert the county that their child would be homeschooled. Once this was done, the parent would hire me to educate their child. I would keep a daily journal of what material was covered and I'd keep samples of student work. (These were legal requirements at the time.)

I began telling friends with young children of my homeschooling plans, setting my starting date for the day after Labor Day, which was two months away. I made a flyer with my fees (materials and tuition), daily schedule, and the subjects I planned on teaching. I had a separate flyer with what I expected from the parents such as sending their children to school fed, rested, dressed and ready to learn with plenty of food to get them through the day.

Within a few days I had secured six paying students for September classes. My personal children were looking forward to having school in the house with their friends.

I set up a small classroom in my home which was, not to brag, completely adorable. There were matching desks with chunky yellow chairs, books, games, a dry-erase board, a dinosaur wall mural, colorful paper chains, and a lot of art supplies.

Hurricane Andrew delayed my opening, as I was without power for a week and my yard was an absolute wreck, but compared to thousands in South Florida who lost everything I fared very well.

The day I started, I had a total of 11 children in my homeschool/learning pod, which included my two boys in diapers. I had activities that all the kids did together and then separate classes for the different age groups, teaching to one set of kids while the other set played. My toddler liked to sit in on our reading circle and my ten-month-old enjoyed sitting in his walker while children took turns reading to him.

I was very busy but happily so. I had the makings of a career, my children were excited (and learning), and my two little ones loved having a house full of kids to play with every day. I was making some money (which my husband let me keep to spend on whatever I wanted).

Professionalism

The most important aspect to homeschooling, or any endeavor for that matter, is to do it as a professional. Even if you are just teaching your four-year-old how to count to ten, do it as a professional would.

I have met homeschoolers who did not approach their activity with a professional standard. Each and every sub-par homeschooler I have met has created a problem for their child. I have seen homeschooled children with no manners, who are socially awkward, behind in skill level or grossly unprepared for the next grade level because of a parent who "half-assed" home education.

One parent took their 12-year-old out of school due to stress, but then gave the child two full years off "to decompress." The boy busied himself with social media but did not do one academic assignment for two years. By age 15 this boy had the skillset of a third grader, which was a big problem as the boy's dream career required an actual education, including college classes.

Another mother only taught math to her ten-year-old for one hour a week because her child did not "connect" with math. I pointed out that I did not have a "connection" to my toothbrush, but I used it several times a day. In the future, this boy may have a terrible time "connecting with a job" when his employer finds out he cannot add, subtract, multiply, or divide.

Yet another homeschooling parent told me that she used to struggle with grammar so it was expected that her child would also struggle with grammar. She was certain her child "inherited this difficulty" just as she inherited her facial features from her father.

I don't think biology works this way. It is not like there is a "defective grammar gene" that runs in the family, preventing one from learning what a noun is.

This is just an excuse not to tackle grammar. And it is a poor excuse at that. If biology did work this way, then only rock stars would give birth to rock stars, and only star athletes would come from star athletes. Her child is being held back by a self-imposed idea that she will never be able to understand the basics of writing a sentence because her mother struggled with grammar. What I see when a parent defends their child's academic struggles is a parent who is blind to their child's actual potential. The parent does not believe their child can do anything but be mediocre or outright fail, so why bother trying.

I know a parent who only assigned academic packets to her young children on Mondays, leaving them to finish everything by the following Friday. The mother justified this practice by saying she was "instilling responsibilities and time management." She was not doing either. Her children were sleeping in until noon and copying work from each other. There would be rightful outrage if a public school teacher only showed up to class on Mondays, leaving her class unattended for the remainder of the week.

I would never ever subscribe to this way of operating. All children need to be directly supervised and properly guided. Period. My personal children were "very good" mainly because I did not leave them any opportunities to be "bad." I was present. I was alert. I was involved.

Part of being a professional is that the job gets done right the first time, so it does not have to be re-done later. If you decide to homeschool or start a micro-school, then please do so as a professional.

Organization and Appearances

"Don't judge," is a statement that makes "judging" seem bad. To judge something means to "form an opinion about or make up one's mind or decide about" someone or something.

Like it or not, one is judged every single day. Opinions are formed based on one's appearance, the state of one's possessions, along with several other things, including the behavior and appearance of one's children.

My personal children arrived at class just as they would have if they attended a traditional school: they were bathed, their hair was combed, their clothes were neat, they were wearing socks and shoes. They each had their own lunchbox full of food. They were not permitted to study in bare feet or roll out of bed and wear pajamas to class.

If you decide to homeschool, your home and classroom should be neatly organized and welcoming. You as the teacher should have an appearance that sets a good example. This has nothing to do with weight or wearing designer clothes. It has everything to do with presenting oneself in a professional manner that is deserving of respect.

My goal in setting up my classroom was that it would be so aesthetic and friendly that it would make one want to be there. While my classroom at home was never featured in a magazine, I never had one complaint from a parent or student about the study space. I created a functional, fun space and maintained it.

Schedule

I cannot stress the importance of setting and adhering to a schedule. This does not just apply to homeschooling; it applies to life. Children should have a set daily routine of breakfast, lunch, dinner, chores, bath time and bedtime, with lots of room for play between.

There should be an exact start and end to each homeschooling day, with exact times for breaks, an exact time for reading, math, handwriting, games, art, singing songs, and other subjects.

A schedule is a must. What time does the day start? When are breaks? What time is reading, writing, math? When does the day end? The only time we'd go off schedule was to go on a field trip, have a holiday party or celebrate a birthday. Otherwise, the schedule was kept in.

I have met people who only homeschool once a week, or who let their children decide when they wanted to do school work. This is sloppy and unfair to the child as it does not prepare them for the real world. The real world runs on exact deadlines and time frames.

For me, school started at 9:00 in the morning and was over at 2:00 in the afternoon. I did 10-to-15-minute academic sessions (seat work) with 30 minutes of puzzles, board games, arts and crafts, and snacks between. The arts and crafts would usually be a project that would support something we were learning about, such as having kids make figures that demonstrate "Life Cycle of a Frog" out of air-dry clay or building a log cabin out of popsicle sticks for Abraham Lincoln.

The discipline of a schedule contributes to the learning process.

Daily Drills

I created a binder I called "Daily Drills." In the binder were pages featuring something specific such as a page listing vowels, a page with the upper case alphabet, a page with lower case alphabet, colors, shapes, words naming colors, days of the week, months of the year, coins, and so on. With today's technology one could easily create this on a computer, but for me, I cut up flash cards and labeled them for the binder.

Every morning I'd spend ten minutes drilling from this binder. For my kindergarten students, I'd point to the letter *f* and say *eff*. The kids would repeat this sound as a group. I'd go through a few letters in this way. Then I'd pick a letter and ask one student to give me the name and sound, going around the room asking individual students to name and say the sound of various letters.

I'd point to a picture of a dime and ask, "*What is this?*" The kids would answer "*Dime!*" Then I'd ask, "*How many cents is a dime?*" And the kids would answer "*Ten!*" If someone did not know or got the answer wrong, I'd simply give them the correct answer then ask the question again so they could answer it correctly.

This binder grew to include states and capitals, the solar system, continents, oceans, time, money, and basic math facts.

Asking children to spell words or go to the board and show the correct sequence of writing a letter such as the two lines needed to make the letter *h* was part of this daily drill.

The kids thought of this as a game. I did not try to review everything. Just a few things for ten minutes a day was good enough to reinforce skills, and I found it an excellent way to start the day.

Learning How to Learn

My success in teaching can be credited to using the concepts contained in the book *Learning How to Learn* based on the educational discoveries of L. Ron Hubbard. The first page of the book boldly states, "You can learn anything you want to learn." This was completely the opposite of what every certified professional said about my son and it got my attention.

While I am not going to do a page-by-page walk-through of the book, I will share the most important aspect of learning: knowing the definitions of the words one is using. When one can define the words of a subject, and demonstrate their use, one will truly *know* the subject and, most importantly, be able to *use* the information.

One of the statements that resonated with me the most was that if one gets to the end of a page and doesn't remember what one read, he or she has gone by words that they cannot properly define.

When I was a kid I was an avid reader. My favorite series was Nancy Drew. But for the life of me, I could not go more than a page or two without blanking out. I picked up one of my old books and sure enough, there were four or five words on each page that I did not know. After I clarified them, I no longer got lost reading.

To further look into the "importance of words," I challenged myself on a walk. I looked at a tree and asked myself, "*What is the definition of the word 'tree'?*" And I answered, "*A plant.*" Well, so is a dandelion and a tree is not a dandelion so I'd have to look up the word "tree" as I could not define it. I saw a car and asked myself, "*What is a car?*" And I answered, "*Something you ride in.*" So is a bus, train, submarine, and an airplane. I'd look up the word "car" when I got home, too. Long story short, I could not provide an adequate definition for anything. I was as dumb as rocks and I was about to start homeschooling! I ended up purchasing several dictionaries and using them almost daily.

I recall purchasing a lesson plan for states and capitals for second graders. The first step was to "Locate the United States of America on a globe." While the lesson wasn't completely horrible it did not define any words.

"United" means together as one. Such as going to the arena to watch the Miami HEAT. We may not agree with the refs or the coaches, but we are *united* in wanting our basketball team to win. In order to understand the word "state" the student needs to know what a border is. Going through all the words, including the word "of" (where the letter *f* is pronounced like a *v*), is key to understanding the subject of the "United States of America." I found that when I defined the words first, my students remained attentive and interested versus when I assumed they knew the words. (Just because one hears or says a word one hundred times a day does not mean that one can define the word.)

Another lesson I did (that incidentally made my students feel really smart) was when we were studying animals. My then three-year-old son could tell you if an animal was a carnivore, herbivore or omnivore as he learned that "carne" meant "meat," "herb" was "plant," "omni" was "all" and "vore" was "eat." Taking the kids to the zoo and asking them to identify the carnivores, herbivores and omnivores was just another step in increasing understanding of the animal kingdom. (Not to mention all the comments we'd get from people walking by who called the kids "little geniuses" because they had such confidence in what they knew.)

In 30 years of tutoring middle school math, the biggest source of confusion was the subject of "fractions." Not surprisingly, over this 30-year period not one parent or child could give me the proper definition of the word "fraction." Not one. There are only a dozen or so words involved with "fractions" and once one knows them and can demonstrate how to use them, the student will have the foundation to master fractions for the rest of his or her life. Fact.

Having the information on defining words became a staple in my teaching. I lead all lessons by defining the basic words of the subject. Math has its own language that when understood makes math actually easy to do.

I highly recommend that one invests in older dictionaries. And until your child has a high school reading level with a good grasp of parts of speech, I do not recommend you require your child to look up words on their own. I find it far better for you to look up and explain words when necessary.

Advice

Do not wait until you have "everything figured out" before you start homeschooling. When I started homeschooling, I did not know what I was doing. I have been at this for over 30 years and am still figuring things out. Learn from mistakes, try not to repeat them, and do things more right than wrong, be a professional, don't give up when "life" slaps you in the face, and you should do okay.

Homeschooling or running a learning pod is hard work. However, it can be incredibly creative and fun. Done well, the reward is stable, productive, moral children with common sense who grow up to be stable, productive, moral adults with common sense.

The only one standing between my son Damon being educated or indoctrinated, labeled, and drugged was me.

The only one standing between your child getting educated or indoctrinated, labeled, and drugged is you.

Chapter 14

Losing a Husband, Adding a Son and Becoming a Private School

Full disclosure. When I started homeschooling Damon, I was on my second marriage with two children from each. (Save your judgments on being married twice before I was 30. I assure you I've heard it all.)

Personally, I considered being a wife and mother an executive position of sorts. I was quite happy to be a stay-at-home mother of four, hoping to one day add a few more to the family. I think raising children and caring for the home to be one of the most important, creative things I could do or have done.

I kept my home clean and organized, managed dentist appointments, handled the money, planned birthdays, wrote thank-you notes, bought curtains, and did all the things one does to run a home. My children were happy, well-behaved, got along very well with each other, and were in my eyes just phenomenal. Each one completely different, yet very much the same (if that makes any sense).

I did not feel "less" because I did not contribute income. I did not feel like I sacrificed my life in the slightest. If anything, I felt empowered.

Thankfully, my ex-husband and then husband set any potential differences aside, adoring the children regardless of whose DNA each carried. The children attended family gatherings, they got birthday presents, and went to restaurants with both sides of the family. When my first husband lost his mother, he asked me to go to the funeral with him which I did without hesitation.

Comparing us to other divorced couples who actively engage in warfare, putting each other down in front of their children or jumping to point out the faults of the other, my situation was really good. We were co-parenting and acted like adults.

Both men were very supportive of having our children taught by me as both witnessed for themselves the downfall of Damon. Therefore, I expanded my "executive" duties to include running a homeschool, which was treated as another hat I wore with separate tasks.

I was really busy, but I really enjoyed the life I was building.

My youngest was maybe eight when my second husband decided he was "done" with being a husband and father. He stopped paying the mortgage, the car, bills, credit cards and refused to take responsibility for any of his family obligations. He drained all bank accounts (including the kids' money) and left to pursue a much better life—whatever that meant. Later he was arrested for drugs, then again for fraud, then again for who knows what.

I understand divorce. I do. But I do not understand how a man (or woman) can just wash their hands of their children, leave like they never existed and on top of that "rob" them of their savings accounts.

Thankfully, my first husband stepped up. He was not asked to, he just did. He did not have the finances to save my home from foreclosure or replace the car that had been repossessed. But he did become a stable father figure to my boys; children that were not biologically his. Every month, if not every weekend, he spent time with them. He bought them clothes, took them to the movies, took them to the best Cuban restaurants and participated in all school events. He never presented me with receipts, asked to be paid back or complained. Guillermo remains a very active part of my children's lives today.

This time period was one of the most stressful I have ever endured. I did not go the "victim" route and spend the day ranting while doing dishes with hostility. There was no point. My father had just been diagnosed with cancer, so I did not go to my parents for help. I was frustrated (an understatement) and remained ultra-focused on my four children who needed stability, not a mother who was upset and venting all the time.

Then, as if I needed any more proof of how drug-driven our culture had become, during an annual medical exam after finding out I was recently divorced and my ex was nowhere to be found, my doctor offered to prescribe me something to quote: "Take the edge off." I politely declined stating that I thought it was in the best interest of myself and my children to *keep the edge on.* The situation I was in required me to be fully on point, not in some drug-induced haze.

I was more determined than ever to make my homeschooling career financially viable.

Most people had no idea what I was going through. I am not known for drama. That said, I had two friends who were just champions: my neighbor Lillian and my friend Kristin. These two women have no idea how much they helped me just by being there.

Lillian and I would be sitting in the shade, sipping lemonade while watching our children play in the pool and laugh ourselves silly planning the revenge on my second husband. (Calm down—it all was a joke.) Our "plans" were more like storylines from old-school cartoons or from the 1960s Batman TV show that involved trap doors over shark tanks. Each "plan" was funnier than the last. One of our best ideas was getting my 12-pound terrier Rocky trained in mixed-martial arts so he could take care of the situation. (We decided against using the dog as he'd be sure to snitch if interrogated.)

Yes, Lillian was definitely a bright spot in my life. Hilarious. Brutal. And a great, great friend.

I began researching family law as it pertained to child support. It took months of filing motions, submitting documentation before finally, after a year, I went before a judge.

My ex-husband was present and verified he had not paid child support, explaining that his grandmother passed away and he was grieving, or he could not find a job, or he got robbed or he went to jail and could not pay and so on. He assured the judge he was "working on a deal" and would catch up shortly. A new child-support agreement was drawn up, signed and on the way out of court my ex-husband said, "Good luck finding me. I'm not going to give you an 'effing dime.'"

My friend Kristin was waiting for me at home, asking me how it went. I burst into tears, sharing the details. All my research, my work, my preparation were for nothing. I was hoping to collect a portion of unpaid child support as I needed it to save my home from foreclosure, but that was not going to happen and what was I going to do and how am I going to pay my bills and blah, blah, blah. After I was done with my rant, my friend said it was her turn.

While I was in court, she received a call from her doctor saying she was ill and most likely would die. She said this to me almost peacefully. As if she were quietly ordering tea in a fancy restaurant.

She and her husband decided she was not going to go without a fight, but as she prepared for her "personal health war," she needed me to take in her youngest son and raise him as if he were my own. (Her mother was going to take in her older boy.) Once Kristin got better, she'd take her sons back; if she did not make it, she'd die knowing both had a chance to experience a normal childhood. In the meantime, she would soon be bedridden with her husband putting in 18-hour days between work, caring for her and medical appointments. This was an unforeseen emergency and she needed me in a big way.

And just like that I stopped crying. My problems were instantly put into perspective.

I was not going to get child support. Period.

I was going to lose my big, beautiful five-bedroom home on a quarter acre of land with a 45-foot-long lap pool. Period.

I was on my own. Period.

Life is not always fair. Period.

And I better get over it. Period.

I was alive. I was healthy. I was needed. And when a dying friend asks you to take her son there is only one correct answer.

Despite the stress I was under, I had to keep it together as a lot of people were counting on me, my children being top of the list. I could not allow myself to lose it, freak out or to break down.

I woke up being a mother of four not knowing that I would go to bed being a mother of five. Funny how things happen, right?

Thor became my fifth and middle child. (Yes, his real name is Thor, though my boys never missed an opportunity to call him Spiderman.)

Thor's mom hung on for years, ultimately relocating to the Midwest to get away from the Miami humidity. Her husband remained by her side through all her treatments. Before she passed, she and her husband thanked me for including Thor in my family, homeschooling him and for giving him three wonderful brothers and a beautiful sister.

I miss Kristin. We were pregnant with our first boys together and when my daughter was born, Kristin just fell in love so decided to have another baby. Exactly one year later Thor was born.

Kristin was truly one-of-a-kind and one of the most intelligent people I have ever known. On the outside, she looked like a woman who would go to a farmers market and talk about seeds. Floppy hat, garden gloves, watering can, socks with sandals, and a dress with large embroidered smiling sunflowers on it. But on the inside, she was a fence-jumping, concert-crashing, head-banging wild woman with an insanely inappropriate sense of humor.

Homeschooling to Private School

It was December 2001 when I was in the thick of the aforementioned crisis that I was contacted by a woman semi-desperate for help with her ten-year-old daughter. Tamara was referred to me by her dental hygienist who had her daughter attending school in my home.

Tamara explained that despite being in one of the best private schools, her daughter Natalie was in the fourth grade and could not read or write one word. Her daughter was passed from grade to grade because she was "tall", and the school administrators felt she should remain with classmates her own size. On top of being academically behind, Natalie hated school and protested the hours and hours of homework, which became a daily fight to get completed.

Tamara had spent thousands on certified tutors and child psychologists with no improvement. A psychiatrist told Tamara that her daughter had a low IQ and would never be able to learn. Medication was recommended so her daughter would not be "so upset" about school and could "be better managed."

I did my own quick assessment, finding that Natalie did not know all the sounds of the alphabet and could not do simple math addition or subtraction.

I showed Tamara the book, *Learning How to Learn*, letting Tamara know we would ensure Natalie could define words and demonstrate things she learns. I explained to Tamara that Natalie had missed basics taught in kindergarten so that would be where we'd start. The work Natalie would be given would start off very simple but would accelerate as her skills increased. There would be no homework, as I wanted Natalie to enjoy her life after school.

Further, my 17-year-old son Damon (well versed in methods found in *Learning How to Learn*) would be Natalie's teacher. All said, I was very confident we could fix the problem.

Tamara's eyes were as wide as they could go. In 20 seconds she was given an educational solution from a non-certified person (me), told her daughter could in fact learn, no homework would be assigned and a 17-year-old boy would be the one to help Natalie learn using study methods found in *Learning How to Learn*.

Understandably, that was a lot to digest, but over to her to decide what to do.

Tamara told her neighbor about meeting me and how hesitant she was with going forward. Her neighbor said: "Well, you've done everything else. I think you'd be crazy not to give this a try."

Natalie joined my homeschooling group after Christmas break in January. A standardized test placed this ten-year-old, fourth-grade girl at a kindergarten level in reading, language arts and math.

After the first day, Tamara asked her daughter how it went. Natalie responded: "If you put me in any other school, I'll run away from home."

Natalie got along well with Damon and her new classmates. Within minutes she was laughing and chatting. True to my word, Damon had Natalie making letters of the alphabet out of Play-Doh. She was counting tiny teddy bears for math and working on proper penmanship starting with tracing letters of the alphabet. Within days her writing improved, and she was reading three letter words like "cat," "mop" and "dig."

Just two months later, Natalie took another standardized academic test, this time scoring at a third-grade level in every subject. Not only did she go up three grade levels in eight weeks, but she was reading books for pleasure at home. Tamara said she took Natalie to the bookstore twice a week as she was so eager to read. By June, Natalie was firmly at grade level, was reading chapter books and had built up quite a library at home.

Tamara could not believe that a 17-year-old (in jeans and a backwards baseball cap) did more for her daughter in a matter of weeks than a small army of certified teachers, psychologists and psychiatrists did in four years.

And that this *miracle* occurred at a dining room table using a dictionary, Play-Doh, tiny plastic bears, and did not involve hours of homework or stress.

It was, per Tamara, completely unbelievable.

Tamara, a stay-at-home mother, approached me privately. While she was ecstatic about her daughter's progress, she expressed concern about the "other girls and boys" who, like Natalie, struggled and were being prescribed drugs because they could not read or write.

The conversation went like this:

Tamara: "*Barbie, you can't keep this to yourself. Do you even realize how many kids need this? Do you know how many parents want exactly what Damon did for Natalie? You have to do more. You need to start a school.*"

Me: "*I know. But that all comes with a price tag that I cannot afford.*"

Tamara: "*I have a crazy idea....*"

Tamara offered to put up a $60,000 personal loan so I could move my activity into a commercial location that would accommodate more students. This figure ended up almost doubling due to permits, zoning and other governmental requirements, but we did it. *She* did it. We took my school from my home and moved it to a commercial location making it an official private school.

Tamara wanted to take on administrative functions such as finance, payroll, and registration. As principal, I would hire staff, oversee the educational programs, do fundraising and PR.

And it worked. As I already had non-profit status, Tamara was able to get us approved for state scholarships that covered school fees for qualifying families.

By the way, Tamara's daughter graduated on time with a 3.65 GPA and went on to college.

In many ways, Tamara is the real hero here.

Because of her insistence to see that more children were helped and her willingness to take a financial risk, we have successfully educated hundreds of children. Children I never would have met had I remained teaching from my home. Children, who like her daughter and my son, were told there was no hope of being able to learn, but who now have mastered academics without the need of labels or drugs.

Chapter 15

Education (Getting It Right Stories)

One does not need a degree to figure out what education should be. One really only needs a dictionary. The word educate comes from the Latin word "educere" from "e (out)" plus "ducere (to lead)." Educate basically means to "lead out."

Education is the process of giving another the information and skills needed to "lead" their life competently.

It is essentially a communication that goes from a trusted source such as a book, coach, tutor, teacher, parent, boss, etc. and arrives to a recipient (student), resulting in the recipient or student fully understanding what came from the trusted source.

A key word here is trusted. Being an authority does not make one a trusted source. The emphasis should be on what actually works. What gets a result.

Education is not cramming information down someone's throat so that it can be regurgitated later. A student who can repeat information to pass a test is not "educated," they are a parrot. Parrots repeat—they do not understand.

Education is not forcing one to accept information without question or telling another what to think. This is how one trains a dog. Sit! Stay! Roll over! are commands to be obeyed. Children are not animals. They should not be "commanded" as animals.

Education done correctly should give one the tools for *how* to learn, *how* to research, *how* to think, so that one can make their own choices, make their own judgments and find their own success.

Education must embrace and take into account the child's individuality, purpose(s) and personal interests. As an example, children interested in sports should play sports and be given reading material on sports and athletes. Children interested in drawing should be given ample opportunities to draw as part of their daily assignments. They should be encouraged to add illustrations to daily assignments or draw pictures to show, for example, that 2 + 2 = 4.

The goal of any educational endeavor is a competent, self-reliant individual who can use the skills learned to solve problems and challenges. This applies to brain surgery just as much as it does to baking cupcakes. Properly educated in either field one should be able to perform brain surgery resulting in a healthy, functioning patient or bake a cupcake that tastes so good it makes the person eating the cupcake want more.

Simply stated: **The goal of childhood education is to provide the child with the skills he or she will need to survive and solve the problems of living; to make study an activity that is both enjoyable and approached with determination, to teach one how to think and act logically; to create independent learners, competent leaders and contributing members of society.**

The following are a variety of actual stories concerning children and adults that illustrate the power of education done right.

Adam, Age 5

Twice before my son Adam was five, wild birds landed on his shoulder. One was a sparrow in Ohio when Adam was four, the other a crow in Miami a year later. Adam greeted each bird with a "Hi guy," as if this was the most natural thing in the world.

Clearly, my son had a gift. His affinity with nature extended to snakes, lizards, frogs and ducks. Wherever Adam went there were raccoons, grasshoppers, cockatoos, and once while fishing with his grandfather, he saw a baby hammerhead shark. (I found out after the fact that much to the horror of his grandfather, Adam jumped overboard to get a closer look at the baby shark.)

To support Adam's interest, I bought him a 55-gallon reptile tank, allowing him to pick out the heat rock, mulch, water dish and three green garter snakes from a pet store. Every two weeks we'd move the sofa in front of the tank and place a fishbowl full of feeder fish in the tank and watch the snakes hunt.

When Adam started bringing home reptiles in distress, such as frogs that jumped in a puddle of motor oil or a lizard that had been mauled by a cat, I bought a second 55-gallon tank to be used exclusively as a hospital. In the case of the frog covered in motor oil, Adam would let the frog swim in a small container of purified water to detox. Adam would feed the frog tiny bugs caught outdoors. The frog would then be placed in the "hospital tank" and be left alone to nap on a heat rock. Adam repeated the process of a detoxifying bath, food and rest day after day until the frog no longer shed a residue of oil. Then I'd take Adam to a park or wooded area where he'd release the frog. I paid him $3 for his work.

Adam's Reptile Set Up · Top Tank for Pets; Bottom Tank for Hospital

Paying Adam $3 per saved animal returned to nature was the perfect solution to not having my home overrun with reptiles. One month Adam's efforts earned him $30. Not once did I have to remind him to maintain his tanks or feed a critter. He was on it.

In school, animals were incorporated into every subject Adam studied. He'd use plastic zoo animals to practice counting, adding, and subtracting. When Adam began reading, his grandparents, aunts and uncles started sending him books about animals. Granted, a few of the books only had one sentence on each page, but other books were more advanced.

As Adam was interested in the material and could use what he was learning, he never lost an interest in reading. By the time he was 11, he had read over 200 books about insects and animals, successfully rescuing dozens.

Homeschooling and Language Arts

I find creative writing to be one of the hardest subjects to teach. Every student has their own level of creativity and trying to tap into their creativity with "writing prompts" doesn't always work.

My eight-year-old son Michael, along with his nine-year-old brother Adam and three other classmates, put their creative writing skills to good use by creating a homeschool newspaper Weekly News, selling each edition for 25 cents.

Weekly News was promoted as cutting-edge journalism. In truth, the main purpose was to make some money while making fun of Damon. Nothing in their paper was true. No facts were checked. Headlines were invented. (Some may say it's kind of like modern journalism.)

The boys would follow Damon around, taking notes: "Damon made a peanut butter sandwich. Story at 11." The illustrations that went with the articles were just as ridiculous. Sales doubled the week Michael learned how to correctly spell "diarrhea." "*It was dark. It was storming. Damon was home alone. There was a knock at the door. It was diarrhea...and it wanted a hug.*"

Ridiculous or not, *Weekly News* became a staple in my homeschool activity, motivating a group of boys to fully embrace language arts as a subject. To this point, Michael was nine when I showed him how to use quotation marks. You would have thought I bought him a new bike he was so excited. He knew that this skill would make his story writing even better.

By high school, both Adam and Michael could write poetry, fiction, and non-fiction essays very well.

Adam wrote a historical fiction short story of what it was like to be a teenager in World War II. It was written in first person and followed the main character having severe anxiety, missing his mother and trying hard not to cry while approaching the beach, gun in hand, on D-Day. The details and pace of the story were near perfection. Adam read his work to his classmates, and one could hear a pin drop.

I feel the hours my boys spent each week pouring their humor into the school newspaper when little kids contributed to their ability to write well as young adults.

Morgan, Age 12

As I have spoken so much about my boys, I think it is only fair to mention a story about my daughter and supporting her purpose. Morgan loved learning and strived to put her best efforts into her schoolwork. She excelled with homeschooling and liked helping younger students learn, especially her little brothers.

Morgan was 12 when she voiced that when she grew up, she wanted to teach professionally. I told her that police officers and brain surgeons needed to be adults, but teaching and tutoring were dependent on skill, not age. She could in fact begin tutoring immediately. It was decided that she would charge $10 per hour and her clients would be five and six-year-olds. She would focus on reading, math, and handwriting.

I bought my daughter a desk calendar and a phone book to keep track of appointments and promoted her services to families and friends that I homeschooled.

Honestly, parents did not expect much. They'd drop off their child and run errands, returning in an hour, paying their $10. The children were happy to work with Morgan and the parents happy for a little break. However, within a short time, parents were saying that their children were actually reading better or could add without using their fingers. Parents were equally impressed at Morgan's communication: "Here is a list of ten words Amanda needs to practice. I suggest you buy some Play-Doh and have her make the words out of clay. She does this with me, and it helps her with spelling."

I did not micromanage my daughter. I did not get involved with her scheduling. I did not get involved with her communication with the parents. It was her business. And my girl shined! She kept a file on each student, showing the parent what they covered and what games they played. If one of her students liked sharks, she'd find a coloring page of sharks to use as a reward. If a student wanted to read about sharks, she'd find a beginner reading book about sharks.

Everything Morgan learned for herself, she used as a tutor. Phonics, math, sentence structure, proper formation of letters and numbers; she used all her skills. Soon my 12-year-old daughter was making from $50 to $80 per week tutoring kindergarten and first graders from home.

By the time Morgan was 15, she had several private students, including children of a Grammy Award winning artist. Morgan worked with this individual's children from their home in Miami for over a year, teaching them alphabet sounds, letter combinations and basic reading and math.

The kids would make up songs using words they'd just learned, they'd play games, and when Morgan drilled flash cards with one, the other one would play with her hair. There were discussions about raising tigers and building time machines. Occasionally the two-year-old sibling would demand to be included and would listen to Morgan read while sitting on her lap drinking from a bottle.

These children (two of the best-behaved, well-mannered, and creative I have ever met) adored my daughter, often calling her "Daphne" from Scooby-Doo or "the Popular Girl!" Bragging: "Our teacher is the Popular Girl. Ohhhh, Morgan is the Popular Girl in town."

And my daughter adored the children. The result of all this mutual love and respect: By ages five and six, both children loved school and were reading at a third/fourth grade level.

Prior to the family going on a world tour, the father reached out to me saying that all his kids talk about is Morgan. He said out of all the tutors and teachers they have ever hired, none came close to the connection Morgan had with his children. And none were able to get them reading or writing so well.

He and his wife wanted to see if Morgan could travel with the family so she could continue homeschooling their children a few hours each day. I was assured she'd be included in family dinners, excursions and have security. They would treat her like one of their own. (This did not work out as Morgan would have been homesick before the plane left the runway. But what an honor for my daughter just to be asked.)

We ended our conversation with him personally thanking me for raising such a wonderful daughter who ended up being a positive role model for his own children.

Ray, 55-Year-Old Vietnam Vet

Ray found out about me through a minister of a Baptist church who became aware I was teaching study skills as part of my homeschooling. Ray was unemployed and considered himself semi-literate. He wanted to improve his grammar and learn how to study. He lived in one of

the poorest areas of Miami, over an hour away by bus, and had no way to pay for tutoring. No worries. I paired Ray with Damon who had just turned 15 and needed community service hours to graduate.

Ray would take a bus to my house twice a week. Beginning with a course on dictionary skills, Damon had Ray read everything

from the book out loud. Any time Ray would hesitate, stumble, or read the wrong word, Damon would help him locate the word or words that Ray did not fully know and get them defined. Once they found the word and the proper definition in a dictionary, they'd trade examples and sentences using the word.

Ray completed over 150 worksheets on parts of speech and punctuation on this course. He started borrowing reading books to take home, ensuring he used a dictionary when needed. It took him three months to finish the *How to use a Dictionary Course*. He said he learned more with Damon than he had in his entire time in school.

The day before my youngest son Michael's birthday, I announced that to celebrate we'd do our normal math lessons in the morning, but afterward the kids could play Monopoly. Ray, who was working with Damon, raised his hand, asking, "Can I get in on that action?" The answer was "yes."

The following day Ray was sitting at my dining room table playing Monopoly with a group of boys. He announced, *"Okay fellas. I came to win."* Forty minutes into the game, Ray had hotels on all the properties in line with Boardwalk and Park Place.

Ray was not messing around. A boy, down to his last dollar, landed on Park Place with a hotel.

The boy asked: "*Ray, are you going to let me slide?*"

Ray: "*No, sir.*"

Boy: "*I don't have enough money. What can I do?*"

Ray (in his deep booming voice): "*Boy, you better get a dictionary and look up the word 'bankruptcy.'*" This was followed by an explosion of laughter from everyone playing the game.

Ray often helped me with my homeschooling students by grading papers, drilling flash cards or reading stories. He continued working with Damon for the following year. He learned basic study skills, grammar, and got help addressing math difficulties.

During the holidays, I did not homeschool, so we did not see Ray. In mid-January, we still had not heard from Ray. Finally in February Ray called saying: "*Hey. I moved. I no longer live in the projects. I got a job in Tampa and have a nice apartment. I really want to thank you for opening your home to me. What I learned with Damon changed my life. And I know what "change" means. (Laugh.) Thank you again. You have no idea how much you helped me.*" He then asked to speak with Damon. I overheard his deep voice say: "*Damon, it's Ray. You still running the place?*" He thanked Damon for being both a tutor and a friend.

What Ray does not realize is that he made a lasting impact on my children, too. They all had good experiences helping him with academics or having him help them. And they still remember the time Ray kicked their asses in Monopoly.

Father G

In the early 2000s, I was homeschooling a little boy who was deemed "unteachable." The boy made a complete turnaround in my care. The transformation was such that his aunt, a reporter for a Telemundo News station, did a full story on how the methods from *Learning*

How to Learn resulted in her nephew excelling in his academics. This story aired in multiple Latin American countries. (Her nephew was seven years old at the time and is now a dentist.)

After seeing the Telemundo feature, Father G, a Catholic priest living in Colombia, had a church official contact me to arrange a meeting in my Miami home. Father G was being assigned to a church in Tennessee that had a large Hispanic congregation. Besides providing religious services, Father G was tasked with finding and implementing a literacy program for children considered "at-risk."

Father G (and a translator) arrived at my home during morning classes. I walked both through my dining room, kitchen and converted garage (now a large classroom), introducing them to children of all ages who were working on various assignments. Father G was thrilled to discover that Damon (like most of my students) spoke Spanish. He asked the kids about what they were working on, and what they liked about being homeschooled. The kids were very receptive, answering his questions.

Father G witnessed Ray (the adult mentioned above) seated with Damon working on a grammar course. Damon showed Father G the grammar study guide, noting that the words, demonstrations, and worksheets were listed in the order to be read and completed; saying that Ray was currently working on verb tenses. Seeing a teenager paired with an adult, in the middle of a house full of children learning, was per Father G, exactly what he was looking for.

He noticed how alert and engaged the students were. He watched them drilling flash cards, doing math, putting together large puzzles, and making the human skeletal system out of Play-Doh. He thought it was particularly clever that the students took turns reading out loud to my dog, Rocky (who loved the attention).

Father G ended up delaying his Tennessee plans a few days so that he could get through the *Learning How to Learn* study guide, which he completed under the guidance of a bilingual volunteer.

Father G found his experience in my home to be very moving. There was friendly simplicity about it all. He was just another study-partnership in a house full of students.

He appreciated that when a child became confused or gave an incorrect answer, the first action wasn't to reprimand or give the correct answer. The first action was to ask the child to define the words prior to the confusion. Seeing for himself that once the words were properly defined, the same child, now understanding what they were reading, was able to work out the correct answer by themself.

As a priest, he said (via translator) that he could use what he learned when delivering church services, especially when relaying scripture, or even reading it for himself. He felt by providing parishioners the meanings of words that they too could be less confused and more able to work things out.

He told me that he felt empowered to not only raise someone's literacy level but to restore someone's faith. He considered my home to be a "house of miracles" and strongly believed that our paths crossed for a reason.

Nate, Age 14

A husband and wife stopped by my school office to inquire about my services. Before the woman sat down, she was in grief and was pulling tissues from her purse. The father explained that they were a religious family and had seven children who were all homeschooled by the wife. About six months prior, one of their teenagers went to the park to play football, like he did with his friends every day. An hour later the police showed up; their son had been killed by a drunk driver.

The wife said she could not function beyond feeding her family. The homeschooling had completely dropped out. The couple felt their other children would bounce back in their schooling, but they were very worried about their son Nate. He was a year younger than the son they had lost and looked like a twin. The boys were inseparable growing up. After his brother passed, Nate, like his mother, shut down.

The parents wanted to enroll Nate in my school, firstly, to get him out of the house and make friends. Secondly, to see if we could help him with academics because he struggled even before the loss.

Nate was an all-American boy. He was a blond version of his mother. He was very respectful, helpful, and fit right in. Though he should have been entering ninth grade, he tested out third and fourth grade in reading, writing, and math (using a TerraNova test).

In keeping with the concept of "learning on a gradient" from Learning How to Learn, I knew if Nate tested at a third grade level in reading, his problem was earlier. It may be something from second grade, or first. He may have missed vital basics in pre-school. I just knew we'd have to go earlier than third grade to solve it.

Now to put this boy on a first grade reading program would rob him of his dignity. Possibly embarrassing him by having him on first- or second-grade material on top of losing his brother would just be cruel and inhumane.

I had a private meeting with Nate, explained that we needed to go earlier in reading. My solution was to have Nate become a reading coach to three students who were all five years old. I would have Nate read three to four books to these children each day. Some books may only have one word on each page, that did not matter, he was to read books to the five-year-olds daily. I gave him a reading log to keep track of all the stories read.

My stipulation to being a "reading coach" was that Nate needed to be able to define every word he had the children read or write. If he read the word "sink" as in "I hope my boat does not sink," he'd have to be able to explain what the word sink means to the five-year-olds. If he could not define the word, he was to ask the teacher or get me. (I did not want him to use a dictionary until his reading ability was stronger.)

Sitting next to the kindergarten teacher, Nate spent 45 minutes a day reading or doing phonics worksheets with five-year-olds.

This activity resulted in him reading about 85 simple books a month. I retested Nate with TerraNova in October (eight weeks after his first test). He was now scoring at a fifth and sixth grade level in reading, language, and math. I moved him to be a reading/phonics coach for my third graders. He did the exact same thing. Under the supervision of one of my teachers, he read stories out loud, kept a reading log, defined words, and explained phonics worksheets.

Making him a "teacher assistant" for reading gave him wins and responsibilities. His confidence in reading affected his other subjects. By the end of the school year, Nate was testing at tenth grade across the boards. Reading, language, and math were all at a high school level. No embarrassment. No tears. No stress. No homework.

He is now a certified accountant, like his father.

Eighth Grade Reading Class

One year I taught eighth grade reading to a small group of teenagers. We read several books that the kids really enjoyed. My timing was slightly off as we wrapped our last book with a week and a half left to the school year. I planned on filling the schedule with an extra math class, but my students insisted on keeping our reading group going.

Adhering to the philosophy of defining words as the first step in a lesson, I explained that the word "castle" is a strong structure that can stand up to attacks. The word can also be used to describe a personal strength and the ability to "stand up" to personal situations despite what life throws at one.

I then asked the students to explain to me what a "castle made of sand" would mean, which they were able to do, offering examples such as getting fired from a job unexpectedly.

I handed each student the lyrics to "Castles Made of Sand" saying that Jimi Hendrix was one of the greatest guitar players of his time. None of my students had ever heard of him. I started the music, and the kids followed the lyrics while listening to the song. Afterward, we discussed the song.

I continued with other songs keeping to the same pattern: define a few words, read lyrics while listening to the song, then discuss.

The kids heard for the first time: "All Along the Watchtower" (by Bob Dylan) and "Angel." Their favorite was "Hey Joe" because of raging drums with melancholy vocals that increased in intensity.

One boy commented that he had no idea a guitar could make those sounds. Another girl asked if I thought her father knew of Jimi Hendrix. I assured her he did. (And he did.)

We moved on to Led Zeppelin. Again, no student had heard of them. We defined a few words, read lyrics and listened to songs. "Babe I'm Going to Leave You," "Your Time is Gonna Come" and "Since I've Been Loving You."

Kids were very impressed by the emotional vocals; however, after listening to the last song, a student commented, *"What's wrong with this guy? He only dates horrible women!"*

Another favorite was Linda Ronstadt's "Long, Long Time" about being in love with someone who does not know you exist. A girl commented: *"I can relate to this every single day!"*

In a matter of days, my students had been introduced to a whole era of music they never knew existed. They heard The Who, Crosby, Stills, Nash and Young, Heart, Queen, The Cranberries, Simon & Garfunkel and the Beatles to name a few.

Reading became the favorite class among these students. So much so that when one of my students was going to miss reading class due to a dentist appointment, her mother called begging me to change the schedule so that her daughter would not miss anything.

Financial Literacy Class

The lesson plan and project that my high school teacher Nancy put together for our financial literacy class was genius. The class was broken down into ten units, one unit for each month, each month focusing on one aspect of finances.

On the first day of class, Nancy had several bowls containing cards, instructing girls to pick from "Bowl A" and boys to choose something from "Bowl B," and so on. The cards determined the student's job, income, and number of children. The girls picked cards containing the name of a male classmate. This was who they would be "married" to for the duration of the year resulting in groans and giggles.

Enough Is Enough!

September's lesson plan was all about financial planning. The class learned about bills and how these differed from expenses. Based on income and number of children, each team was given a deadline to submit a complete list of monthly bills and expenses.

We had students visiting the local insurance agency for various quotes. Kids went to the grocery store to list items with prices, and kids went online searching for the cost of housing. By the end of September, everyone had turned in their work.

Again, words were defined, and assignments given to use what was learned. Students teamed up to make public service announcements about identity theft, or they had to maintain a mock checking account. One month Nancy did a lesson on inflation using chocolate chip cookies that the kids really enjoyed.

What the kids were not prepared for was that at the beginning of each month, I would show up to class holding a bowl containing my own index cards. In October I announced that a hurricane was coming.

The look of horror on the students' faces was priceless. Each team would pick one card to see how the hurricane affected their lives. Cards stated things like "No damage caused." "Power went out causing a $500 loss in groceries." "Your fence was destroyed." "A bedroom window was broken." "A tree totaled your car." "Your dog escaped, bit a neighbor and you are being sued." And my favorite, "Your mother-in-law lost her home. She has medical needs, two cats and is moving in." The students then had to figure things out, such as how much it cost to hire an attorney or replace a fence.

Every month the teacher took up another topic, and every month I showed up with another bowl of random occurrences that happen in real life. Sometimes a team would pick, "You got a $1,000 bonus!" "Your company went out of business." Or "You broke your ankle playing tennis." (I think one of my sons picked something about backing into a car and causing $750 in damage. The girl he was partnered with said: "You are such an idiot. Learn to drive!")

By the end of the year, the students had learned about credit cards, bouncing checks, inflation, insurance, balancing a checkbook, handling financial emergencies, and more. Real skills for real life.

History Lesson on Primary Source Comes to Life

In the study of history, a primary source is a first-hand account of what was actually occurring at a particular time period. If one wanted to know what it was like to see the first Beatles concert one should ask someone who was actually there.

Personal journals and original documents provide information as it was actually viewed or experienced. This is vastly different from secondary sources, that re-tell events, sometimes hundreds of years later, that frankly, may or may not be accurate.

As my school is in a mall and about 50 feet from a gym, a group of about 18 senior citizens would sit outside the school drinking Cuban coffee after their morning gym class. They'd stop in and share coffee with my teachers, and we'd share leftover birthday treats with them. This relationship went on for months.

My high school kids were learning about different types of governments (socialism, democracy, communism, etc.) and their impact.

Acting on a bright idea, the high school teacher and I put together a special government project. The students had to write ten questions that would be used to interview said senior citizens about their lives. In other words, the kids would get first-hand accounts, for example, on what it was like to grow up in Cuba.

The high school teacher approved the students' questions before the interviews took place. The kids' questions were along the lines of: Where were you born? What government did your birth country follow? Did your family agree or disagree with government policies? Explain. What age were you when you arrived in the United States? What was the most challenging thing at that time? And so on.

The senior citizens were thrilled to be asked to participate in a government project. On the day of the event, groups of students and adults could be found inside the school and at tables and benches outside the school. With clipboards and questions in hand, the kids sat and asked these senior citizens to tell their stories.

My students met a couple who spoke about him being jailed and her being pregnant and not seeing each other for years. Another gentleman was just four when he fled to America with his mother following the murder of his father. Another spoke of how his wealthy family lost all property and bank accounts. Some of the people talking were

the same age of the students in my school when their lives were torn apart.

Along with the horrific stories were stories of persistence, of family, of faith in God, of survival, of not giving up, of building back, of goodness, of hope in America.

There is no textbook on Earth that comes close to what my students learned and experienced that day. There was emotion. There was respect granted from both sides of the table.

The class discussions because of this "bright-idea project" were heartfelt and intelligent. I know it impacted the adults as well. They sincerely thanked me for letting them each tell their story. And for providing such a receptive audience of wonderful young people.

These stories, and hundreds more like them, truly show the impact of "education done right." The student wins. The teacher wins. And as a society, we all win.

Saving my own son was just the beginning. Deciding to homeschool, then expanding this activity into a small private school has aligned my role as a mother, an artist and a teacher perfectly.

Nothing compares to a child who absolutely loves school and is an active participant to their education.

Listening to a six-year-old read their first book; helping a middle schooler understand how to solve a pre-algebra problem in such a way that they'll understand it for the rest of their life, or having a high school graduate (previously deemed unteachable) show up having become an honors student with a nursing degree are stories that never get old.

And this is why I love what I do.

Chapter 16

The Bigger Picture and Bringing Back What Worked

Prior to the introduction of 20th century psychology and the adoption of the philosophy that "man is but an animal and should be conditioned to obey," and before textbooks were mass produced by corporations owned by world bankers, and before multiple choice was introduced, and long before children were branded with labels such as "Attention Deficit Disorder," "Gifted," and put on drugs, America was a literate country. The American education system, while not perfect, was working. Just Google an eighth grade academic test from 1930 to see how far the educational standards have fallen.

I look at my 1970s public school first-grade experience compared to what happens to today's first graders and I'll take the 1970 education without hesitation. There were no standardized tests, no checklists, and no homework. The focus was on reading, proper formation of letters and words (handwriting), and arithmetic (counting, simple addition, and subtraction). Science was purely a hands-on activity of collecting leaves, learning about animals, seasons, and weather. We were not expected to stay seated all day.

We practiced manners, sang songs and were busy with arts and crafts. We had 30-minute recess before and after lunch, where we'd play group games under the guidance of our teacher. Subjects like spelling, grammar, language arts and social studies were not taught until higher grades.

And guess what? We graduated first grade able to read, able to write, able to do math and ready for the next grade. My six-year-old classmates were not drugged for "immature drawings" or labeled by psychologists or other so-called experts for behaviors that are normal childhood behaviors. Despite the billions spent on modern education, my first grade from 1970 was a highly enjoyable experience and far more effective than the first grade "pressure cooker" of today.

This bears repeating: First grade in 1970 was far more pleasant and effective than first grade now. My evidence: I loved school. I was not on drugs. I could read, write and do math. I took pride in my work. I looked forward to school as I knew I was getting smarter by the day.

Was it too much to ask that my son have a similar experience? Seriously, was I crazy for expecting my healthy, alert, "normal" son to be able to do what children have been able to do for thousands of years: to learn? Was this really such an unreasonable or unrealistic request?

Was there a time when first graders being able to read was the norm? Was there a time when the majority of students from all grades were literate?

Well, there was such a time.

When was American Education the Best? When was American Literacy the Highest?

I find the following quote about the educational system in the early 1900s (before the "experts" took over) to be very telling.

"In 1910 the literacy rate was so high it was predicted that the public schools will in a short time practically eliminate illiteracy." The Trojan Horse in Education by Samuel L. Blumenfeld. His book is an exposé on the NEA (National Education Association) published in 1984.

Blumenfeld arrived at this conclusion from an issue of James McKeen Cattell's weekly publication "School and Society" dated January 30, 1915. This article lists the year and reported literacy levels of children aged 10 to 14 for several years.

- 1900 reported 42 children out of 1,000 could not read or write (95.8% literacy rate);
- 1910 reported 22 children out of 1,000 could not read or write (97.8% literacy rate);
- 1915 several states reported only 1 child out of 1,000 could not read or write. (99% literacy rate).

Remember that in 2022, the U. S. Department of Education reported that 54 percent of American adults were at or below a sixth grade level in literacy. Using the same scale as above, this translates to 540 adults out of 1,000 who cannot properly read or write, or only a 46 percent literacy rate for our country.

This. Is. A. Disaster.

A Plan to Turn the Disaster Around

In order to resolve this massive problem it is not necessary to reinvent the wheel. The "wheel" already exists. For the past four years, I have collected over 400 textbooks, lesson plans and workbooks from 1930 and earlier. These are the books that were used when America's educational system was considered the best in the world. My collection includes textbooks for: reading, handwriting, cursive, civics, spelling, phonics, arithmetic, science, grammar, geography, history, language arts and readers for kindergarten to eighth grade.

Each book has a section written for the teacher, giving the purpose of the textbook, background information, and suggested use of lessons contained in the book.

Several books caution the teacher on introducing formal textbooks to children under fourth grade as it was believed that overwhelming students in first, second and third grade with information they could not easily process would result in the student losing their natural desire to learn and explore. This would turn learning from an exciting venture to one of drudgery, thus robbing the child and the teacher of the joy of learning.

Another viewpoint expressed in several of these early American books was that the purpose of school was to prepare the student to effectively handle the responsibilities of being an adult. If education was done correctly, the student would grow to be an intelligent, quick-thinking entrepreneur with leadership qualities. Education done right would result in strong families, strong leaders and being right with God and/ or having a strong moral compass.

Several texts from this time period state if academic materials were thorough enough, and the difficulty was increased on a slow gradient—focusing on mastery rather than speed—the child should be able to progress through the subject on his own with minimal teacher interference.

The following are quotes from a couple of the antique textbooks I have collected:

1930 *THE NEW DAY ARITHMETICS FOURTH YEAR BOOK* (Grade Four)

"Aims are mastery rather than inaccuracy and uncertainty. Lower aims in arithmetic cannot be justified.

The greatest waste in arithmetic lies in half learning then forgetting."

Charles E. Merrill (author)

1863 *NATURAL SERIES PRIMARY ARITHMETIC FOR SCHOOLS* (Grade Three)

"The danger in teaching any elementary subject is falling into a habit of monotony (lack of variety, boring) which soon robs both teacher and student of nearly all the interest they would otherwise feel in these studies.

"In order to secure thoroughness, give short lessons, and spend much time in daily review. If in the exercise of 'fours,' [multiplying by fours] *do not proceed until everything that came before is as familiar as the alphabet. If it requires one month, take it, if one year, the time cannot be better spent."*

S.A. Felter, Author

A phonics textbook from 1935 warned the teacher against "modern reading protocols," citing that teaching reading via phonics was proven to be an effective method and should not be replaced with "whole-word" learning.

Seat work in kindergarten was limited to 10 percent of the school day, meaning most of the day was devoted to moving and exploring. Very little of the kindergarten class had to do with pencil and paper. Further, kindergarten was not academic. Students did not learn to read or write in kindergarten. Students learned how to work in groups (social skills), following directions, manners. Kindergarten was intended to prepare young children for formal education which began in first grade. Even then, seat work for first graders was low—meaning kids were not working on packets for hours on end. Instead, the teacher was to keep the students interested in learning through stories, songs, and games. (This was very close to the stress-free first grade I experienced.)

I could go on. The takeaway from my library of early American textbooks is that back when we were a literate nation, our educators were not chanting "test scores, homework, learning disabilities, and drugs." Instead, they presented information in a simple, interesting way, slowly increasing the difficulty, so students could master skills, apply what they learned, and successfully enter the next grade.

My goal is to bring these books back to life. Not just the books, but the educational philosophies behind the books. A time when public schools produced a 97 percent literacy rate amongst American children.

Can you imagine the impact of an effective math program that took a student from counting to five to algebra? A thorough math program that progressed slowly, ensuring the student both mastered and retained skills? A program that was built upon and included the correct definition of words? Now imagine this being created for phonics, spelling, language, grammar, civics, geography, science, the Constitution, Human Rights, and history (just to name a few).

Such a curriculum could accommodate a learning pod of four children, a private school of thousands or, dare I say, an entire nation. For families wanting to homeschool, it would solve the problem of not knowing where to start.

The result of implementing such a curriculum would be that today's generation would be correctly educated. The parent or teacher delivering the curriculum would also benefit as their post-1930 education would be repaired.

The only educational field that may remain untouched by psychological agendas are cookbooks. The most popular and best selling cookbooks on the market today offer simple definitions of terms, clear illustrations, step-by-step instructions and are easy to understand. Simplicity does not mean lower standards. (I don't think Betty Crocker would be an advocate for cooking with a 70 percent accuracy.) Simplicity means the reader can effectively produce an outstanding meal. Every. Single. Time.

Can you imagine what effect a "Common Core cookbook" would have? Kitchens nationwide would be burning to the ground.

Having simple, effective and thorough materials (for all subjects) that aim for mastery would be a game-changer for our children. If my son Damon was given 20 or 30 simple, fun worksheets he could color that drilled the letters *b*, *d*, *g*, *p* and *q* by a teacher who believed in him, I guarantee he would have sorted out his confusions of these letters. How do I know this? Because this is exactly what happened after I worked with him.

Damon was never "mentally handicapped." He was never "dyslexic." He never needed mind-altering medication to learn. He needed a teacher who genuinely loved children and a day full of crafts, singing songs, group games and simple materials that covered beginning reading, writing and math that gave him wins, not losses. My son would have thrived in my 1970s first grade classroom. My first grade teacher would have adored him.

How many other children, and adults for that matter, have been incorrectly labeled and medicated because of faulty, confusing textbooks?

How many good teachers change professions because they were forced to use complicated materials, abide by psychological philosophies and were not permitted to effectively teach?

The educational authorities, psychologists and psychiatrists are not going to solve "education." Their allegiance is with the pharmaceutical companies, who have turned "struggling students" into a billion-dollar industry that pushes drugs and offers no cures.

The politicians aren't going to solve "education." Especially considering that pharmaceutical companies are among the largest campaign donors.

Advances in technology and children being raised on devices haven't come close to solving "education." If anything, the dependency on devices has crippled the minds and creativity of our youth.

I feel by returning to the workable philosophies and texts of the early 1900s we can once again create a nation of literate, successful, strong individuals who become intelligent, competent, stable leaders.

I am 59 and have no wish to retire any time soon. That said, my time on Earth is limited. The task of creating complete materials and lesson plans based on these early 1990s materials for kindergarten to eighth grade may be daunting, but is, in my opinion, exactly what is needed for more children (and adults) to master the skills needed to live their life happily, competently, as leaders and contributing members of society.

I successfully educated my children.

The same thing can be done to successfully educate yours.

If I can do it, so can you.

Chapter 17

What's Next?

What's next? Well, I am not done. That's what's next.

This book came about because of three different conversations, with three different friends, at three different time periods. All involved me expressing how unbelievably disappointed I was in the school system and what was happening all around me.

Yes, I turned my homeschool activity into a private school, hired like-minded people and we have helped hundreds of children. I love my staff. I really enjoy my students and I feel I have had an amazing career.

But it just is not enough.

Every single day some desperate parent shows up needing help with their nine-year-old who cannot read or their teenager who can't add. While I was working on this final chapter I met the mother of a second grader who cannot read. She placed her little girl on Prozac and Adderall, presumably as a "solution."

This makes me feel like I have the only house standing after a hurricane. While I am happy I survived the storm, I cannot ignore the fact my neighbors are suffering.

Same goes with education. I am happy my children were raised and educated well, but I cannot ignore all the children suffering in the hands of a school system that let them grow up thinking that they, the children, will never be "good enough" or "smart enough" and that they, the children, are the problem.

So, there is more to do. I am not done.

Getting The Word Out

My first step was to write *Enough is Enough!* as I strongly believe that parents of children struggling in public schools need to know that the problem is most likely the school and not the child. Getting this book distributed broadly enables me to reach parents on a scale I would never be able to do in one-on-one consultations from my office at my school.

I understand that the information contained in these pages may be hard to digest, but I feel it is far harder to come to realize that your high school son is going to miss out on a baseball scholarship because he cannot read well or multiply "six times three." (True story of a family I interviewed recently who were seeking a "fast solution" for a 17-year-old who was issued a calculator in the second grade and is now failing high school.) There is no "fast solution" for ten years of bad, or perhaps no, education. It's actually heartbreaking; here is a decent career-minded boy who has virtually no chance of learning ten years of English and math before he turns eighteen.

This book is the "who," "what," and "why" behind the failing American education system. Now that we know what happened, the next logical step is to put in writing what can be done about it and then how to do it.

A Homeschool & Learning Pod Handbook

As I said in chapter 13, homeschooling is no joke and not something one should embark upon lightly. Despite the many obstacles I faced when I decided to homeschool Damon and my other kids, I pushed forward and built my own homeschool program. Yes, there were bumps and set-backs. But ultimately I put together a workable system for my homeschool and learning pod which later grew into what is now my private school, H.E.L.P. Miami.

For my next book, I am going to write a guide that I wish had existed when I started homeschooling. I am going to share everything I have learned from the last 30 years in educating children in a simple, story filled handbook.

In it I will cover how to establish and run a homeschool activity, or a learning pod, with information such as what subjects to teach, what schedule I found workable, and what resources I found useful (or useless). It will include how to keep a child interested and engaged, what I did when my child was disinterested or disengaged, as well as the records I kept, daily reports I filled out and what I expected from the families who enrolled their children with me.

After this homeschooling "How to" guide is complete, I will make a complete list of what subjects should be taught and what skills should be mastered for each grade level, based on the advices found in my collection of textbooks from the early 1900s. (Remember, these are the materials that were being used when our public schools were graduating students with a 97 percent literacy rate.)

This too will be simple and straightforward.

For example, kindergarten subjects will be phonics, math, games, manners and crafts. Kindergarten students will be expected to be able to recognize the letters of the alphabet, write letters and numbers, and count to 20. Writing book reports or doing a presentation on how Gerald Ford became president (an actual public school assignment for a five-year-old) would not be part of kindergarten. Seat work would be restricted to 10 percent of the day, with the rest of the time spent on group activities, such as singing songs, playing games, being read to and learning about nature.

Cursive handwriting would be introduced in second grade with the goal being that the child be able to correctly form capital and lower-case letters and write simple sentences in cursive, with evenly spaced, neat penmanship. Mastering multiplication tables up to the 12s will be listed as a third grade skill, with the majority of third grade focusing on the drilling of multiplication tables, while maintaining skills learned in earlier grades. Students would start diagramming sentences in the sixth grade and so on.

Having an outline of what subjects should be taught at each grade level and a list of skills to be mastered for each subject will provide parents and teachers with known objectives to work toward. Again, this is something I wish I had when I was starting out.

While having a complete outline of skills for kindergarten to eighth grade would be very useful, it still places a major burden on the parent or teacher to find sane, simple texts for the student to use.

It is fine to say third graders need to learn multiplication tables and seventh graders need to know the basics of the U.S. Constitution, but where does one obtain simple materials to teach this? Where does one purchase a workbook that goes over multiplication using simple definitions of words and progresses slowly from 1 x 1 to 12 x 12 with ample repetition contained in worksheets? Where does one find verbal drills resulting in a child who knows their times tables? Where is the lesson plan and text that gives clarity (with simple definitions of terms) to the Constitution as the foundation of our country?

These materials do not currently exist. At least not the way I envision they need to be.

And this brings me to my ultimate "solution." The thing that makes educating one's own child not only possible but doable.

Project: Restore American Literacy

In chapter 3, The Takedown of American Education, I pointed out a startling fact about the quality of education provided in our schools in the early 20th century: American schools at that time graduated students with a 97 percent literacy rate!

When I discovered this fact some years ago, I engaged in research to try and discover what was being taught in schools at that time that was different from today. Much of what I learned is provided in this book. I also began a process of acquiring and reviewing key textbooks from that era in many subjects such as phonics, handwriting, math, word usage, spelling, grammar, creative writing and more.

The fact is, there was a time when our schools produced literate students on a regular basis. At that time, the American school system was the envy of the world!

This work led me to conceptualize what I am now calling Project: Restore American Literacy. I use the word 'restore' intentionally as it implies returning something to a previous, better condition. In this case, the previous better condition I envision is one which uses a curriculum derived from our most successful educational era minus all the nonsense and destructive elements added in later (as I describe in this book).

Publishing my book *Enough Is Enough!* is the first step of this project. Parents, students, educators, policy makers and others need to know the information in this book. Knowing that our schools were once successful and what derailed that success, I believe, is vital to restoring American literacy.

The homeschooling handbook is the second step in Project: Restore American Literacy.

The third phase of Project: Restore American Literacy is broader and more encompassing. A few years ago I started to collect textbooks from the early 20th century. My goal is to develop a complete curriculum for kindergarten to eighth grades based on these earlier, successful materials. It will focus on mastering basic academic skills.

I know from my personal experience that every child has the innate ability to learn and to master these skills when given simple but workable materials and properly taught without unproductive additives like labeling and pharmaceutical medications.

I also know from my experience in training others to successfully teach children, that most adults I worked with had themselves gaping holes in their own education. This was not a barrier as long as they had a detailed lesson plan to follow that included definitions, examples and discussion points.

Independent Castle Publishing Initiative

My goal is to provide a homeschooler with complete grade level materials (texts, workbooks and lesson plans) taking the guesswork out of what to teach. This curriculum will be published by a company I formed called Independent Castle. It will produce and publish sane, simple workbooks, textbooks and lesson plans that address all of the grade level objectives for kindergarten through eighth grade. The materials will be designed with an easy learning gradient so as to achieve mastery of skills as the goal.

For example, math would start out in kindergarten with sorting and counting objects, writing numbers 0 to 10, identifying money, adding to 10 and subtracting from 10. A child who successfully graduates kindergarten math will be able to take on first grade easily and continue mastering harder and harder skills until they are competently able to problem solve at an algebra level.

Illustrated workbooks will be accompanied by simple lesson plans for the parent or teacher to follow. This will provide definitions of words and usage examples and demonstrations for the student to do, such as using toy dinosaurs to show "5 take away 2 is 3." Games and suggested reading books will be named as part of the lesson.

Creating materials in this fashion for each grade for phonics, hand-writing, math, word usage, spelling, grammar, creative writing, manners/life skills, government (the Constitution), science, geography and the arts has many benefits, such as:

- The materials will give the parent or teacher a stable point from which to homeschool. In 32 years, one of the biggest concerns I hear from parents considering homeschooling is "What do I do?" or "Where do I start?" This would no longer be a problem.

- Children will be correctly educated (not indoctrinated). Children completing this curriculum will enter high school well-versed in reading, writing, grammar and math. They would not have "gap-ing holes" in their education.

- The materials will be formatted in such a way that adults using them with children will themselves have "wins" teaching, even if their own education has weak areas. Personally, I have sorted out my own prior confusions on math by teaching it, using a defini-tion-oriented, step-by-step approach. I did not let my children know that I did not master "fractions" until I was almost 30, but that is what happened. One of my current teachers (her first language is Spanish) was thrilled when she sorted out the correct usage of "their, there and they're." Overcoming prior academic confusions is a positive "side-effect" of teaching correctly from workable materials that are simple and make sense.

- With these materials complete I will be able to design a secondary program for semi-literate teenagers and adults who struggle with reading, grammar and math.

- The proposed materials could very well save our country as we'd be producing literate, fast thinking teenagers who become leaders and productive, contributing members of society.

The key to this is simplicity. The materials should easily walk someone from one skill to the next. As soon as a subject such as learning the sounds of the alphabet, for example, becomes so complex that only a so-called "expert" can teach it, we lose. (Notice that all of the billions spent on master's degrees and psychology have not produced a literate society.) I say we skip the complications and just return to what worked.

H.E.L.P. Miami School

Another integral part of my plan concerns my school, H.E.L.P. Miami. To be very blunt: the school cannot die when I die. My school was created because I was in desperate need of a solution for my son. I have gone from teaching at a dining room table while bouncing a toddler on my lap, to setting up a learning pod in my garage to be able to teach more children, to expanding into a full kindergarten through 12th grade school in a storefront in a local strip mall.

My vision is for this school to become a model for teaching children as I have outlined in this book. It could serve as an example that can be replicated in schools across the country, whether based in homes, storefronts or churches. Using this model school, parents would be able to effectively cut ties to government-run schools, until such time as these schools reform their current practices.

To realize this goal will require me to secure a campus and greatly enlarge my team. My vision is a welcoming school building with a flag pole at its entrance, on a property that is several acres with a playground, a basketball court, a theater space, library, cafeteria and plenty of big, beautiful classrooms for 100 or so students in grades K to 12.

This model school will be set up so that others who wish to see the Project: Restore American Literacy vision in action can visit and learn. It will provide a place to pilot the new materials that will be generated from the Independent Castle project as well as a teacher training curriculum I will develop to create competent, creative educators bypassing the need for expensive and lengthy training to get college degrees.

In Summary

We do not need to waste any more time pointing fingers at what went down in the past. I believe the American people no longer trust the child psychologists and psychiatrists or so-called "experts" anyway.

The bottom line is that we as a country cannot ignore the fact that today many, many children are graduating high school unable to read or do basic math. We cannot ignore the fact that today in our schools children are being labeled "mentally handicapped" and prescribed mind-altering medication at an alarming rate.

A different and effective alternative to that kind of education is needed.

I am a successful educator because I completely bypassed the failing education system I describe in my book. I can help others have the same success by creating effective, simple, definition-based materials and lesson plans for K-8th grade.

I strongly believe that this Project: Restore American Literacy is the long-term answer.

As you might imagine, all of this is a massive endeavor. In particular, my Independent Castle initiative is a huge undertaking. I am committed to completing it as rapidly as I can. However, with outside support, allowing me to put additional resources into the project, I can get the work done much faster.

Stay Connected and Informed

If you're interested in more information about Project: Restore American Literacy, the Independent Castle initiative, or want updates on my upcoming homeschooling handbook, I invite you to visit my website at www.BarbieRivera.com. Your support means a lot to me, and staying informed is the first step.

If you were inspired by my stories, or you'd like to share your experiences, please don't hesitate to reach out. In addition to my website, you can connect with me on social media for regular updates and discussions about education.

Follow me on X at www.x.com/BarbieEducator and Facebook at www.facebook.com/BarbieRiveraEducator/.

The input and support of friends, new and old, are invaluable to me. I look forward to hearing from you.

Acknowledgements

The book would not have occurred without the following:

Frank for telling me over 30 years to "stop whining (about the school system) and do something about it" encouraging me to homeschool, then "politely insisting" I start a private school, then telling me there is still much more to get done. Your directness is both inspiring and hilarious—but here I am an author!

Tom and Massimo for encouraging me to write my story.

Suzanne and Jen for being Suzanne and Jen.

And to the team that fell into place.

Chris Latham I don't think an actual title exists that encompasses all that you did for this project. I appreciate you very much.

Nancy Gurliaccio for proof-reading every word, and proof-reading again when I changed my mind, and proofreading AGAIN when I changed my mind back.

John Stanard for first agreeing to look over my work as a friend. Then taking on a senior editor role (which was just fantastic). Then becoming a project manager which included giving me ideas on two additional books. I am very grateful for your "two-cents" and attention to detail.

Kris Nickerson of Brilliance Learning Press for walking me through the publishing process and formatting my story in such a beautiful way.

And finally to Miss Anne Sullivan for setting such an amazing example, giving me the courage to effectively help my son.

About the Author

Barbie is an artist, mother, speaker, homeschooling advocate, founder of a private school (H.E.L.P. Miami) and author. She lives in Miami, Florida with her two dogs: Franklin, a basset hound and Remington Begonia (Remi), a tricolor dachshund.

Made in United States
North Haven, CT
02 June 2024